# The MAILBOX®

The Education Center®

grade
**Preschool**

# Arts and Crafts

THE BEST OF
The MAILBOX®
MAGAZINE

The best arts-and-crafts activities from
the 1998–2004 issues of *The Mailbox*® magazine

✳ **Easy Art Tips**

✳ **Fall Activities**

✳ **Winter Activities**

✳ **Spring Activities**

✳ **Summer Activities**

✳ **Anytime Activities**

✳ **Timesaving Index**

**Managing Editor:** Kelly Robertson

**Editorial Team:** Becky S. Andrews, Kimberley Bruck, Sharon Murphy, Debra Liverman, Diane Badden, Thad H. McLaurin, Karen A. Brudnak, Juli Docimo Blair, Hope Rodgers, Dorothy C. McKinney

**Production Team:** Lori Z. Henry, Pam Crane, Rebecca Saunders, Chris Curry, Sarah Foreman, Theresa Lewis Goode, Greg D. Rieves, Eliseo De Jesus Santos II, Barry Slate, Donna K. Teal, Zane Williard, Tazmen Carlisle, Kathy Coop, Marsha Heim, Lynette Dickerson, Mark Rainey, Sheila Krill, Amy Kirtley-Hill

## www.themailbox.com

©2007 The Mailbox®
All rights reserved.
ISBN10 #1-56234-756-X • ISBN13 #978-156234-756-7

Manufactured in the United States
10 9 8 7 6 5 4 3 2 1

# Table of Contents

# Easy Art Tips

## No-Spill Glue

Do you have "no-spill" paint cups in your room? In addition to filling them with paint, fill some of them with glue. It's easy to squirt glue in the holes in the rims, and the snap-on lids keep the glue from drying out. Best of all, children can use paintbrushes to apply glue to their projects so that there's less mess! Storage is easy, too. Just stack 'em up!

Ellyn Soypher
Chizuk Amuno Preschool, Baltimore, MD

## Painting Tip

Painting a lunch bag is easy when you insert an empty, rectangular tissue box into the bag. The box makes the bag easier to manipulate and easier to paint on all four sides. It also keeps the bag upright while it is drying.

Linda Gilligan
St. Hedwig School, Naugatuck, CT

## Placemats for Play Dough… and More!

Don't toss your old wall calendar when January first rolls around! Instead, laminate the pictures and use them as placemats for classroom activities, such as play dough, painting, and pasting. Neat!

Bobbie Edwards
Jewish Community Center Preschool
Dallas, TX

## Glitter Bag

Love glitter but hate the mess? The answer to neater glitter application is in the bag! Pour about a half cup of glitter into a gallon-size zippered plastic freezer bag. Then have a child paint glue onto the project to which you want to add glitter. Place the project in the bag with the glitter, seal the bag, and have the child give it a shake! Then remove the item and give it one last shake over a trash can. Much neater!

Irene Miller
WSOS Child Development Program
Elmore, OH

## Cupcake Liners? Neat!

When doing a painting project, squirt the paint into paper cupcake liners. The paint stays put and at cleanup time, you can toss the liners into the trash! For added fun, use colored or patterned cupcake liners for seasonal or holiday projects.

Andrea Henderson
Jefferson Brethren Preschool, Goshen, IN

## Hold On!

Minimize the mess of painting three-dimensional projects with the help of some well-placed clothespins! Simply clip a wooden clothespin onto the object to be painted; then have the child hold on to the clothespin as she paints the object. Ah…less mess!

Beth Lemke, Heights Head Start
Columbia Heights, MN

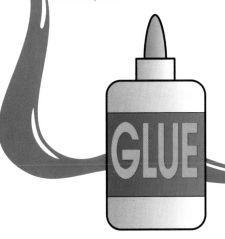

I'm the apple of your eye! Jaime

### The Apple of My Eye

Got your camera ready? These adorable apple frames make a great gift for someone special, such as a grandparent. Take a close-up picture of each child; then trim the developed pictures into circles sized to fit in the center of a small paper plate. To make one frame, sponge-paint a paper plate red. Next lightly sprinkle red or clear glitter on the wet paint. Program a construction paper leaf with "I'm the apple of your eye!" and the child's name. Glue the leaf, a paper stem, and the photo to the dry plate as shown. Complete the frame by attaching a strip of magnetic tape to the back of it. Smile!

### Shiny Shakers

Add a little polish to craft time with these shiny apple shakers. To make a shaker, paint the backs of two small paper plates red. When the paint is dry, brush a mixture of two parts glue and one part water on the painted side of each plate to create a polished look. Allow the glue mixture to dry. Bend a brown pipe cleaner in half; then tape it to the rim of the unpainted side of one plate. Glue a green construction paper leaf near the stem. Position the plates together so that the unpainted sides face each other. Glue the plates together, leaving an opening near the stem. Insert approximately ten dried beans in the opening; then glue the opening closed. Complete the shaker by squeezing a happy face on one side using a mixture of two teaspoons black powdered tempera paint and four tablespoons white glue.

Melba Clendenin
Chester Elementary School
Chester, IL

## Awesome Apples

For a colorful display, try these translucent apples. To make one apple, draw a simple apple and stem outline on a piece of white paper. Tape a piece of clear plastic wrap or a resealable plastic bag over the drawing. Squeeze white glue along the outline; then press yarn onto it, making sure to include the stem to create a loop. Allow the glue to dry. Next tint glue with red, yellow, or green food coloring. Use a paintbrush to paint a thick coat of the glue on the plastic, inside the dried yarn. Let the glue dry for a day. Peel the apple decoration from the plastic; then suspend it. Apples, apples everywhere!

## Apple Buddies

'Tis the season for apples! So invite youngsters to make these apples that can be worn as nametags or sent home for use as refrigerator magnets. To make one, trace apple and leaf shapes onto craft foam. Cut out the shapes; then glue them together. To give the apple a worm buddy, push a green pipe cleaner through the back of it. Thread a number of cereal pieces onto the pipe cleaner; then push the end of the pipe cleaner back through the front of the apple. Twist the pipe cleaner's ends together at the back of the apple. Finally, use a permanent marker to personalize the apple and to add a face to the worm. If a child wishes to wear his apple, twist the remaining ends of the pipe cleaner around a button, through a buttonhole, or onto a belt buckle. Later, attach two strips of magnetic tape to the back of it to make an apple magnet to send home.

## "A-peel-ing" Apples

You can count on little ones really tearing into these apples! To make one, tear a 9" x 12" sheet of red construction paper into pieces. Glue the resulting apple peels onto a precut apple shape (cut from a nine-inch square of white construction paper). Tear a stem shape from brown paper and a leaf shape from green paper. Glue the stem and leaf in place, and the apple is ready for display.

Kellie Shaner-Gordner
D & K's Youngland
Hughesville, PA

## Bloomin' Apple Trees

Real apple trees bloom in the spring and their fruit ripens in the fall. This apple tree craft blooms and ripens right before your eyes! Provide each child with a construction paper apple tree. Then invite her to use a red bingo marker to dab circles on the treetop. When the ink is dry, have the child use a brown crayon or marker to add apple stems. Next, have the child turn over her tree and glue on crumpled pink and white tissue paper squares to represent blossoms. Hang each child's tree in your room and you'll have a crafty orchard of blooming apple trees!

## Acorn Artwork

Display these giant acorns around your classroom to welcome autumn! For each child, cut out a dark brown construction paper acorn, light brown construction paper acorn cap, and two construction paper leaves in fall colors (see illustration). Have a child dip a small rectangular sponge into brown paint and make prints on her acorn cap. When the paint is dry, have her glue the cap, acorn, and leaves onto a sheet of yellow construction paper. Then have the child use a brown marker to add stems to the leaves. Now, watch out for squirrels!

Bonnie Cave
Duluth, GA

## Falling for Leaves

Have youngsters create colorful fall foliage to hang in front of a sunny window. To make one leaf, fold a piece of red, yellow, brown, or orange construction paper in half. Cut out one half of a simple, symmetrical leaf shape, starting at the fold. Then cut out the center of this shape, leaving an outline about ½ inch wide. Unfold the outline; then lay it on a slightly larger piece of waxed paper. Drizzle a generous amount of glue along the shape's outline and in the center of the waxed paper. Press tissue-paper squares onto the glue. When the glue is dry, peel the leaf off the waxed paper. Trim around the leaf's edges. Hang the leaf in front of a window.

Betsy Ruggiano
Featherbed Lane School
Clark, NJ

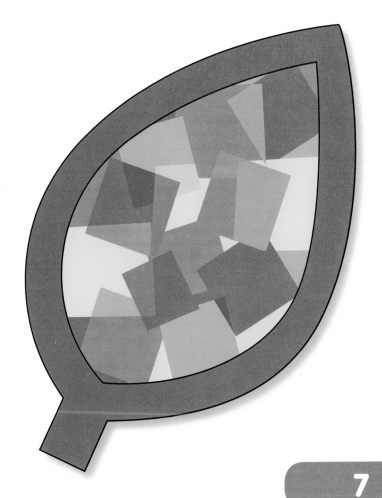

## Ahhh...Autumn!

These autumn leaves are lovely—and easy to make! To prepare, cut simple leaf shapes from tagboard (at least one per child). Next, use kitchen graters or pencil sharpeners to grate crayons in autumn colors into paper cups. Lay a leaf shape on a covered work surface. Have a child take a pinch or two of crayon shavings and sprinkle them onto her leaf shape. Then lay a sheet of waxed paper over the shavings and press the leaf with a hot iron (the child should be at a safe distance from the iron). Oooh—how pretty!

Carol Hammill
Community Christian Preschool
Fountain Valley, CA

## Leaf Lantern

Take your class outdoors to collect leaves; then preserve the autumn foliage with these simply beautiful lanterns. To make one lantern, place two 18-inch sheets of waxed paper on a newspaper-covered table. Sandwich a number of leaves between the sheets of waxed paper. Cover the waxed paper sheets with a layer of newspaper; then use an iron on low heat to join the sheets. Next fold two 4" x 18" strips of fall-colored construction paper in half lengthwise. Slip a folded strip over each long waxed paper edge; then staple the strips in place. Staple together the short sides of the waxed paper to form a cylinder. Punch two holes in the top of the cylinder; then twist one end of a pipe cleaner through each of the holes to make a handle. Invite each child to take her lantern home to share with her family.

Karen Gremer
Walnut Creek Presbyterian Christian Preschool
Walnut Creek, CA

## Winter Preparations

Squirrel away a class supply of brown paper-towel tubes in preparation for this project. To make one tree, cut a hole out of the center of the tube as shown. Also cut slits from the top of the tube toward the center. Bend the tube's sections downward to resemble tree branches. Crumple small pieces of orange, yellow, and red tissue paper; then glue them to the branches. Color a copy of one of the squirrel patterns (page 96); then cut it out. Put glue on the back of the pattern; then insert it into the tube so that the squirrel's face can be seen through the hole. Press the pattern in place. Looking for nuts? Look in this tree!

Virginia Nickelsen
YAI/NYC Early Child Learning
William O'Conner School, Brooklyn, NY

## Fall T-Shirts

These seasonal T-shirts are lovely and leafy! In advance, ask each child's parents to send in a light-colored T-shirt. Then take your class on a walk and have each youngster collect two or three autumn leaves that are not too dry. Back in your classroom, spread a child's T-shirt flat on a tabletop; then slip a sheet of waxed paper or thin cardboard inside the shirt to prevent paint from bleeding through. Squirt some autumn-colored fabric paint into a clean Styrofoam tray. Then have a child use a paintbrush or her fingers to spread paint evenly and thinly over the vein side of a leaf. Have her lay the leaf carefully on the shirt front and then lay a paper towel over the leaf and press. Remove the paper towel and the leaf to observe the leafy impression. Continue with other colors and shapes of leaves as desired. Beautiful!

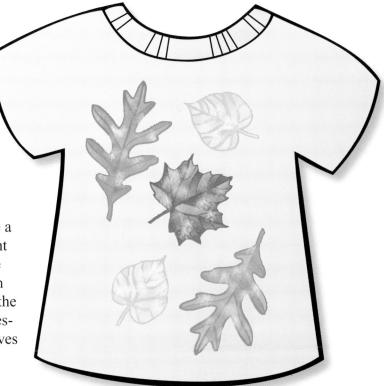

Cindy Bormann
Small World Preschool
West Bend, IA

## Moonlit Autumn Trees

"Whoooo" wants to make these autumn tree sculptures? Your preschoolers will! To prepare, cut a small circle from yellow construction paper and a brown owl shape (pattern on page 96) from brown construction paper for each child. To make one tree, lay five craft sticks on a piece of waxed paper; then paint the sticks with brown tempera paint. When the paint dries, turn them over and paint the other sides. Then use craft glue to assemble the sticks as shown. Glue the yellow moon to the back side of the treetop and glue the owl to the lowest branch. Then tear small pieces of red, yellow, and orange construction paper to make leaves. Glue the leaves on the tree branches where desired. Finish the sculpture by pushing a bit of play dough or clay into a film canister or small paper cup. Then anchor the tree trunk in place.

## Puzzle-Piece Tree

If you have a jigsaw puzzle with missing pieces, this is the project for you! Have each child draw a tree trunk and branches on a sheet of construction paper. (Draw the trees in advance for younger children.) Provide pieces from an old jigsaw puzzle, the kind with a few hundred pieces. Have each youngster glue puzzle pieces to the branches of her tree to resemble the colorful leaves of autumn. Encourage each child to add a few "leaves" falling from the tree or lying on the ground to complete the seasonal effect.

Doris Porter
Aquin System Preschool
Cascade, IA

## Mr. Scarecrow

All it takes are a few simple craft materials to create this scarecrow cutie! To prepare each project, precut a circle face from tan construction paper, a hat from any color construction paper, and a sunflower shape from yellow construction paper. From fabric scraps, cut two small hearts for cheeks, a triangle for a nose, and a hatband. To assemble the scarecrow, glue raffia strips to each side of the face to make the scarecrow's hair; then glue the hat to the top of the head. Glue the hatband and flower in place. Glue a black pom-pom to the center of the sunflower. Attach two sticky-dot eyes and glue on the fabric nose and cheeks; then use a black crayon to draw a mouth. Hello, Scarecrow!

Bonnie Martin
Hopewell Country Day
Pennington, NJ

## Sunny Delight

Light up your classroom with a display of student-made sunflowers! In advance, cut several potatoes in half. Trim some of the halves to make petal-shaped prints and some to make square prints. To create a sunflower, dip a square printer into brown paint; then repeatedly press it onto a large sheet of art paper, creating a somewhat circular design. Outside this, use a petal-shaped printer and yellow paint to encircle the brown area. When the paint is dry, cut around the flower shape. To turn a bulletin board into a patch of sunny sunflowers, staple each student's blossom atop a green paper strip embellished with some green paper leaves. That's sunny all right!

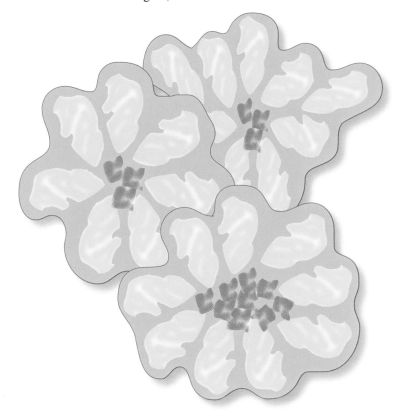

## Hoot! Hoot!

Transforming a brown paper lunch bag into a roly-poly owl is easy and fun! Open the lunch bag and stuff the bag half full of crumpled newspaper. Then fold down the top of the bag and staple along the fold. Next, color a black dot (pupil) near the center of each of two 1½-inch white construction paper circles. Glue each circle inside a cupcake liner. Glue the liners to the front of the folded flap and glue one edge of an orange construction paper triangle to the back of the flap to make a beak. There you have it! A cute-as-a-button bird!

## Baby Owl

To make a baby owl, have a child pull apart a few cotton balls and tuck the cotton into all the nooks and crannies of a pinecone. Help her attach sticky-dot eyes. Then have her glue on a triangular beak cut from orange construction paper or felt. Display the owl by gluing the bottom of the pinecone to a branch or stick.

Cheri Anderson
First Presbyterian Church Day School
DeLand, FL

Lynn Morgan
Corkscrew Elementary
Naples, FL

## Pumpkins on the Vine

This "hand-some" painting project features a mighty fine vine! For each child, use a green marker to draw a curvy line across a sheet of white construction paper. Have a child make a fist and then dip her fingers into a shallow bowl of orange tempera paint as shown. Next, help her press the painted part of her fist onto the green line to make a pumpkin shape. Have her repeat this process to make a few more pumpkins along the vine. Then encourage her to finish the picture by using green paint to make thumbprints for pumpkin stems and leaves.

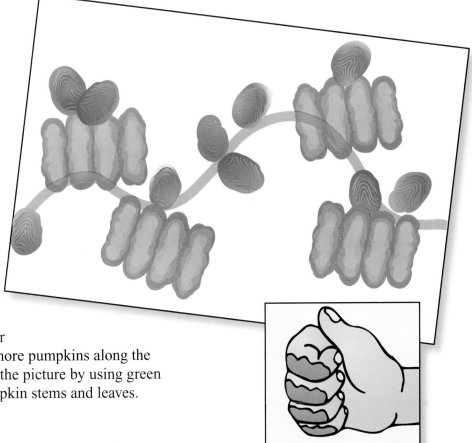

Sarah Booth
Messiah Nursery School
South Williamsport, PA

## Jack-o'-Lantern Mobiles

Your preschoolers will be pleased to make this unique patch of jack-o'-lantern mobiles. To make one, cut out the center of a paper plate and discard it. Paint both sides of the remaining plate rim orange. To make the jack-o'-lantern face, cut three triangles and a zigzag smile from black construction paper. Cut two three-inch lengths and one six-inch length of brown yarn. Glue the features to the yarn as shown. When the glue is dry, tape the yarn lengths to the back of the plate so that the shapes are positioned as desired. Punch a hole near the top of the plate; then tie on a length of yarn so the completed mobile can be suspended from the ceiling.

Cathie Sarvis
Park Avenue School
Wilmington, NC

## Ticklish Bats

These bats look "vonderful" on bulletin board paper murals or T-shirts. To create a bat, paint the bottom of a child's foot. Use black fabric paint if the print will go on a shirt or washable black tempera paint if the print will go on a mural. Have the child press his footprint onto the fabric or paper; then wipe his foot clean. Paint the child's other foot. Help the child press this print so that the heels overlap as shown. Wipe the foot clean. When the paint is dry, use fabric paint (on the shirt) or regular paint to make ears, eyes, and a mouth.

Jan Wicker
First Presbyterian Preschool
Roanoke Rapids, NC

## Flipped Over Bats

Everyone is sure to have a good "bat-itude" when making these creatures. To make one bat, paint a cardboard tube black or brown. Set the tube aside to dry. Using the wings pattern on page 97, make an oaktag tracer. Use white chalk to trace the wings onto black or brown construction paper; then cut them out. Also cut out two small triangles from black or brown paper to represent the ears. Glue the wings and the ears to the tube as shown. Then attach a pair of sticky-dot eyes. Feeling batty? Display these projects upside down!

Laura Castro
Vallco Child Development Center
San Jose, CA

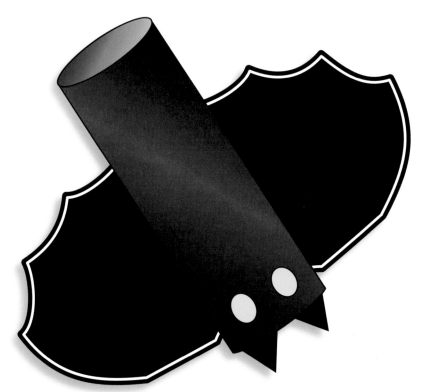

## Coffee Filter Bat

Little ones will go batty for this cute craft! Begin by using a hole puncher to punch out two small circles from white paper. Use a black pen to make a dot in the center of each one. Glue the resulting eyes to a large black pom-pom. Glue on a short length of rickrack trim to make the bat's mouth, as well as two small paper triangles for ears. To make the bat's wings, color a coffee filter with a black marker; then fold the filter into a triangle. Dip the points of the triangle into water. Unfold the filter and allow it to dry. Fold the dry filter in half to make a half circle; then use a twist-tie to gather the folded filter in the center. Use craft glue to attach the prepared pom-pom to the twist-tie at the center of the wings.

Mary Jo Hanson
The Blair Early Learning Center
Altoona, PA

## Haunted House

There's nothing scary about making this Halloween house! In fact, it's "spookily" easy for your little spirits to create. Use the pattern on page 98 to prepare oaktag tracers. To make one house, use white chalk to trace one of the patterns onto black construction paper; then cut along the resulting outlines. To embellish this house, glue on cotton-ball spirits and add some thumbprint ghosts using white paint. If desired, add die-cut pumpkins or pumpkin stickers. Arrange the completed houses together on a display to create a spooky neighborhood.

Mary Hilditch
Relax Children's Center
Baltimore, MD

## Glowing Ghosts

Ooooh…eerie! These ghosts glow, my dearie! To make a treat bag, use glow-in-the-dark or fluo-rescent paint to paint handprints onto a handled paper gift bag. When the paint is dry, use a mark-er to add features. Fill these bags with ghostly goodies that will disappear quickly!

Jami Haarz
Scribbles Child Care
Lapeer, MI

**Spider, Spider**
*(sung to the tune of "Bicycle Built for Two")*
Spider, spider,
You are a friend I know.
You eat bugs that
Eat little plants that grow.
You're not so very scary.
You're not so very hairy.
You have eight feet.
Your web is neat,
Little spidery friend of mine!

## Not-Too-Spooky Spider

Not even Miss Muffet could run away from these spiders! To make one, use black tempera to paint the sides and bottom of a foam cup. When the paint is dry, bend eight four-inch pipe cleaners in half. Then, working your way around the painted cup, gently poke one end of each pipe cleaner leg into the cup as shown. Glue two fuzzy pom-pom eyes on what is now the top of the cup and glue a piece of yarn to one side of the cup to make a mouth. Your eight-legged pal is ready to take a spin! To add to the fun, teach little ones a spider ditty such as the one shown.

adapted from an idea by Judi Silver
Robbins Nest
North Brunswick, NJ

### Dancing Spiders

Hang these dancing spiders from your classroom ceiling and watch the wiggling, jiggling, and giggling begin! For each child, cut from black or brown construction paper a five-inch circle, a three-inch circle, eight 1" x 6" strips, and one 1" x 2" strip. To make one spider, accordion-fold all the strips. Glue the short strip between the paper circles so that the smaller circle (the spider's head) appears to "pop out." Glue the eight remaining strips to the back side of the larger circle, four on each side, to serve as spider legs. Attach two hole reinforcement eyes to the spider's face and draw a smile. Punch a hole in the top of the spider and thread a 15-inch length of string through the hole. Tie the string in place; then hang the spider from your ceiling. Watch out—it's wiggly!

Christy J. McClellan
Song Woods School
Waynesboro, PA

### "Spider-ific" Webs

Put your round cake pans to creative use to make these painted spiderwebs. To make one web, cut a black construction paper circle to fit in a cake pan. Place the paper in the pan; then pour a spoonful of white tempera paint onto it. Next place a Ping-Pong ball in the pan. Gently tilt the pan repeatedly to roll the ball through the paint, forming a web design on the paper. Remove the ball; then sprinkle silver glitter over the wet paint. Carefully remove the resulting web and let it dry. Glue a plastic spider onto the web. Or tie a length of white yarn to a spider, punch a hole near the edge of the web, and then thread the yarn through the hole and tie it off. Charlotte herself would be proud of these webs!

Sharla Park
Friends and Neighbors Preschool
Lehi, UT

## Marshmallow-Print Monsters

There's nothing scary about these monsters. In fact, they're softies! To prepare, squeeze a different color of tempera paint onto each of three paper plates and insert half of a drinking straw into each of three regular-size marshmallows. Then, to make a monster, randomly paint marshmallow prints onto a 12" x 18" sheet of white construction paper, using a different marshmallow to apply each paint color. When a desired effect is achieved, allow the paint to dry. Then trim the paper into a monster shape. Use hole reinforcements, construction paper triangles, and pom-poms to add desired details. There now, isn't he adorable?

Heather L. Miller
Creative Play School
Auburn, IN

## Mummy Madness

Your little ones will go mad for these marvelous mummies! To make one, cut out a copy of the pattern on page 99. Using a glue mat to protect the tabletop, spread white glue that has been thinned with a small amount of water onto the cutout. Cover the glue with torn strips of white tissue paper or toilet tissue to resemble a mummy's wrappings. Cut two black eyes from construction paper; then glue them on the mummy's face. Mount the completed project on an orange background.

Christa J. Koch
Circle of Friends
Bethlehem, PA

## Fine-Feathered Holder

This fine-feathered Thanksgiving project holds plenty of treats! To make one holder, cut six inches off the top of a brown paper lunch bag. Cut six 2" x 5" strips of brown construction paper. Fringe-cut each strip along one long side. To both the front and back of the bag, glue three strips (fringe down) so that they overlap slightly. Bend the fringe upward. Cut a head, a beak, a wattle, a tail, and two eyes from construction paper; then glue them in place as shown. Fill the completed holder with desired treats.

Renee E. DeAngelo
The Rainbow School
Plains, PA

## Flying Turkeys!

To make a hanging turkey project, tie a knot at one end of a length of yarn. Poke a hole in the center of the side of a large Styrofoam cup; then, starting inside the cup, pull the yarn through the hole. Poke colorful craft feathers into the cup as shown. Finish the turkey by gluing paper eyes and a paper beak to the end of the cup. Hang these turkeys where they are safe from the cook!

Helen K. Dening
Silver Creek, NY

## Flock of Turkeys

You'll hear lots of oohs, aahs, and gobbles when you display these turkeys all over your room. In advance, collect a class supply of clear milk jugs. Make sure all of the jugs are thoroughly cleaned and dried. Also cut several construction paper feathers and a simple paper turkey head (pattern on page 100) for each child. To make a turkey, mix a small amount of soap into a three-ounce paper cup of brown tempera paint. Have a child pour the paint into a jug, replace the cap, and then shake the jug until the inside is coated with paint. On each of the child's feathers, write a different thing for which he is thankful. Have the child glue the feathers onto the back of the jug. Then have him add details to the turkey head to glue onto the front of the jug. To finish his turkey, a child glues paper scraps or attaches pieces of colorful tape onto the jug. Gobble, gobble!

Julie Erickson
Red Cliff Head Start
Bayfield, WI

## "Hand-some" Thanksgiving Card

Fingers become feathers for this holiday greeting card. For each child, cut out a simple turkey head and body shape (about ten inches high) from brown construction paper. Write the message shown on each child's turkey cutout. Next, have each child decorate a 5" x 8" piece of tagboard with your choice of spin art, bingo markers, paint, or markers. When it's dry, turn the tagboard over and trace the child's hands. Cut out the hand shapes and arrange them behind the precut body to look like feathers. Have the child draw eyes, a beak, and a wattle on the turkey and add her name below the message.

Cheryl Helaire
Monarch Nursery School
Wolcott, CT

## Thanksgiving Placemat

Prepare these placemats for your Thanksgiving feasts; then send them home as gifts along with Happy Thanksgiving wishes. Write or type the poem shown; then make a copy for each child. To decorate one placemat, glue a personalized copy of the poem onto a large piece of construction paper. Use washable paint to paint the palm and thumb of a child's hand brown. Paint her fingers various colors. Have the child press her hand onto the construction paper. When the paints are dry, have her use markers to add legs and feet, an eye, a beak, and a wattle to her print. Laminate the placemat for durability.

Shelly Dohogne, Scott County Central
Sikeston, MO

This isn't just a turkey,
As anyone can see.
This very special turkey
Was made by hand by me!
Happy Thanksgiving!

Katy

## Gorgeous Gobblers

It takes a few days to make these fine-feathered fowl, but it's time well spent! To make the feathers, use washable tempera paint to make random handprints on a 12" x 18" sheet of white construction paper. Then set it aside to dry. Repeat the painting process for two more days, using a different color of washable paint each day. When the final coat of paint dries, cut to round the edges of the paper.

To make the body, fingerpaint a dinner-size paper plate brown. When the plate is dry, trim it to resemble a turkey's body as shown. Attach hole reinforcement eyes and a beak and wattle cut from construction paper. Then glue the body to the feathers and glue two extra long yellow construction paper turkey legs in place. Now there's a gobbler that's ready to strut its stuff!

Dorathy Reed
Noah's Ark Nursery School
Burlington, WI

## Tree Topper

Top off your tree with these ornaments. To make one ornament, cut a triangle from poster board. Stack and glue cardboard puzzle pieces onto the triangle. When the glue is dry, paint both sides of the ornament green. While the paint is still wet, sprinkle glitter onto the puzzle pieces. Tape a loop of ribbon to the back of the ornament for hanging.

Karen Sheheane
Killearn United Methodist Preschool
Tallahassee, FL

## Foil Christmas Tree

Each of these trees is unique when decorated by your crafty youngsters. For each child, cover one side of a cardboard triangle with green floral foil (used to wrap pots) or foil wrapping paper (used to decorate doors). To complete his tree, a child glues a paper trunk to the back of the triangle and a star to the top. He then embellishes the tree with various art supplies, such as paper scraps and stickers.

Lois Maiese
Camden County College Child Care Center
Blackwood, NJ

### Christmas Bells

Ring out the good news. These bells make adorable gifts! To make one bell, sponge-paint a two-inch clay flowerpot red, green, or white. Sprinkle glitter onto the wet paint. Then glue a child's picture onto the bell and outline the picture with dimensional fabric paint. Allow the paint to dry. Next thread an 18-inch piece of ribbon through a large jingle bell's loop. With the ends of the ribbon even, tie a large knot in the ribbon about one inch above the jingle bell. Starting from inside the pot, thread the ribbon's ends through the drain hole. Pull the ends upward until the knot reaches the drain hole. Tie a second knot just above the hole. Tie the ribbon's ends together.

Peggy Witman
Willow Creek Learning Center
Poland, OH

### Puzzle-Piece Wreath

Got a jigsaw puzzle with some missing pieces? Then you've got the basis for these merry wreaths! For each wreath, cut an O shape (three to four inches in diameter) from heavy cardboard. Staple a loop of ribbon to the cutout to be used for hanging the finished wreath. Then have a child glue on at least three layers of old puzzle pieces, covering the entire cutout. When the glue is dry, paint the wreath green; then glue a red bow to the bottom of the wreath. Have the child use red puffy paint or red glitter glue to add berries. Be sure to add the child's name and the date to the back of each wreath because parents will be hanging these crafty creations on their trees for years to come!

Kelly Nardi
Black Rock School
Thomaston, CT

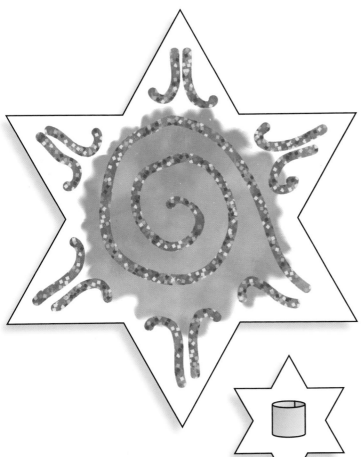

## Star Light, Star Bright

Invite youngsters to top their holiday trees with these sparkly stars! To make one, lay a flattened coffee filter atop a thin white paper plate. Color the coffee filter with washable markers (blues and greens work well). Then use an eyedropper to drip water over the filter, making the ink spread into unique designs. Remove the coffee filter to see the design left behind on the plate. Allow the plate to dry. Cut it into a star shape; then add squiggles and lines of glitter glue in a color that complements the ink. Hot-glue a tagboard ring to the back of the star (as shown) and it's ready to top the tree!

Carol Hargett
Kinderhaus III
Fairborn, OH

## Decaf Santa

Ho! Ho! Ho! To make one of these Santas, cut a six-inch triangle from red construction paper. Glue the triangle to a flattened coffee filter as shown. Glue cotton balls onto the top and bottom of the hat. Use markers to add facial features to the filter; then trim around the edges to create Santa's beard. Jolly good work!

Shelly Wooldridge
Smithville Elementary School
Smithville, WV

25

## Handy Santa

These handy-dandy Santas make great parent gifts! Provide each child with a golf ball–sized ball of white Crayola Model Magic modeling compound. Have the student flatten the ball into a thin pancake. Then trace each youngster's hand on the modeling compound with a pencil. Use the pencil point to make a small hole near the base of the palm. Allow the modeling compound to air-dry overnight. Have each child cut out her hand shape. Mark each cutout as shown. Then have her use markers to color Santa's hat and draw a face. Supply each child with two large cotton balls. Instruct her to pull the cotton balls into several pieces. Then have her glue cotton pieces to the cutout to complete the hat and make a moustache and beard. Tie a six-inch length of ribbon through the hole to make a hanger. Now, sit back and watch Santa hang around for the holidays!

adapted from an idea by Diane Bonica
Deer Creek Elementary
Tigard, OR

## Rudolph Magnet

Round up some cardboard puzzle pieces to transform into reindeer magnets! To make one, use craft paint to paint three puzzle pieces brown. When the paint is dry, glue the pieces together as shown. Also glue on two construction paper eyes and a pom-pom nose. Attach a self-adhesive magnet to the back as shown.

Karen Sheheane
Killearn United Methodist Preschool
Tallahassee, FL

## What Dear Reindeer!

Family members are sure to treasure these Rudolph wall hangings! To make one, paint a cardboard cake or pizza circle with red tempera paint. Using two different shades of brown construction paper, trace a child's shoe on one color and both his hands on the other. Cut out the shoe and hand shapes; then glue them to the painted circle as shown. Add sticky-dot eyes, a red pom-pom nose, and a merry red bow. Hot-glue a picture hanger to the top of the back and your gift is complete. How neat!

Cheryl Songer
Wee Know Nursery School
Hartland, WI

## Nose So Bright!

Even a nighttime blizzard can't stop Rudolph's bright red nose from leading the way! Squeeze white tempera paint onto a paper plate and provide a clean and empty 20-ounce plastic soft drink bottle. To make a blizzard of snowflakes, dip the bottom of the bottle into the paint and randomly stamp it onto a sheet of black construction paper. Repeat the process until a desired effect is achieved. Then dip a red pom-pom into glue and press it onto the painted paper. Santa's on his way!

## Celestial Sensations

To make an angel, trace a child's hands onto white construction paper; then cut them out. Spread glue onto both hand shapes and a Styrofoam cup; then sprinkle on silver glitter. When the glue is dry, invert the cup and glue the hand shapes to it to represent wings. Insert a craft stick into the bottom of the cup, leaving about one inch sticking out of the cup. Press a 2½-inch Styrofoam ball onto the stick for the angel's head. Glue sticky-dot eyes and yarn hair onto the ball. Top the angel with a glittery pipe cleaner halo.

Sandra Anzaldi
Noah's Ark Day Care and Kindergarten
Haverhill, MA

## Angelic Art

To prepare, cut a class supply of seven-inch-tall triangles from inexpensive lace fabric and three-inch circles from white or skin-toned construction paper. Have each child glue a triangle body and a circle face onto a sheet of construction paper as shown. Then have her press her hands into white tempera paint and onto the paper to make the angel's wings. Have her use crayons to add facial features and glitter glue to add a halo. If desired, copy the poem shown for each child and have her glue it to the bottom of the angel.

I'm just a little angel,
So sweet and heavenly,
Made from lace and handprints
For all the world to see!

Sarah Booth
Messiah Nursery School
South Williamsport, PA

## Sweet-Smelling Gingerbread House

Construct a candy-covered gingerbread house without using a single baking pan or a drop of frosting! For each child, precut a simple house shape (similar to the one shown) from tan construction paper. Then provide a supply of scented stickers showing all kinds of candy and treats. Have the child peel and stick to make his house look and smell yummy!

Dana Smith
Baton Rouge, LA

## Gingerbread Kid

This seasonal craft is full of fun and fine-motor practice! To prepare, trace around a large gingerbread boy or girl cookie cutter on brown craft paper two times. Cut out the shapes, stack them, and use a hole puncher to punch holes around the perimeter. Invite a child to decorate one of the shapes by sticking on white paper reinforcements for hair and sticky dots for buttons. Have him add sticky-dot eyes, tiny bows, pipe cleaner pieces, or any other decorations as desired. Restack the shapes and have the child use a long length of white yarn to lace the shapes together. To add a seasonal scent, slip a cotton ball sprinkled with cinnamon between the two shapes before the child laces the final holes.

Mickie Clements
Young Ideas Preschool
Newton, IA

## Dandy Candy

'Tis the season for these pretty peppermints! To make one, have a child paint red and green alternating stripes on the rim of a small white paper plate. After the paint dries, help the child wrap the plate in a piece of clear plastic wrap or cellophane. Then twist the ends of the wrap and tie a length of red curling ribbon around each one.

Michelle LeMaster-Johnson
Windlake Elementary
Milwaukee, WI

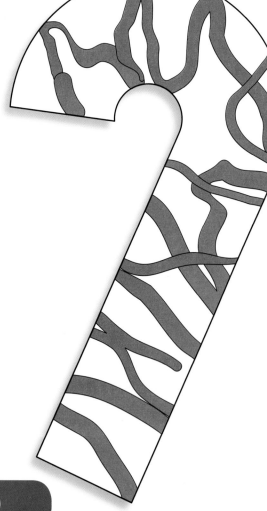

## Peppermint Pretty

This cute candy cane smells as good as it looks! To prepare, add a few drops of peppermint extract to some red tempera paint. Cut a candy cane shape from white construction paper for each child. Working with one child at a time, place a candy cane cutout in a box lid. Put a bit of the peppermint-scented paint in each corner of the lid. Then drop in a Ping-Pong ball. Have the child tilt the box lid back and forth to make the ball roll through the paint and over the candy cane cutout. Look—stripes!

Christa J. Koch
Circle of Friends School
Bethlehem, PA

Sonya Bussan
Third Presbyterian Head Start
Dubuque, IA

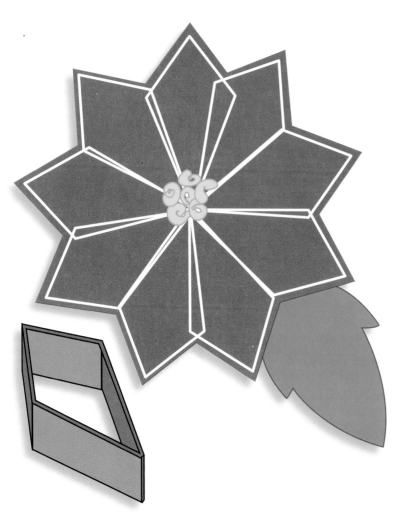

## Painted Poinsettias

These painted poinsettias are a pretty way to add color to your classroom decorations. To prepare to paint one, use an X-acto knife to cut a 2" x 10" strip of corrugated cardboard. Bend the strip in half; then bend two inches of each end toward the center. Tape the ends together to make a kite shape. Dip the shape into a shallow pan of white paint, and then press the shape onto the center of a sheet of red construction paper. Continue printing in a circular fashion, making sure the bottom point of the shape remains in the center. When the paint is dry, glue crumpled yellow tissue-paper pieces to the center of the prints. Trim around the poinsettia shape; then add a construction paper leaf.

Lisa Desrosiers
Gates Lane School of International Studies
Worcester, MA

## Holiday Candle

These pretend candles will make super centerpieces for holiday tables! To make one, first paint a toilet tissue tube with red tempera paint. While the paint is wet, sprinkle on iridescent glitter; then set the tube aside to dry. Meanwhile, glue several 5" x 5" squares of green tissue paper to a small paper plate as shown. Glue a few clusters of small red pom-poms (holly berries) onto the green tissue paper. When the paint on the tube is dry, tuck small pieces of yellow, orange, and red tissue paper into one end to resemble a flame. Then glue the opposite end of the tube to the center of the paper plate.

Carrie A. Gross
Davis Child Care Center
Oshkosh, WI

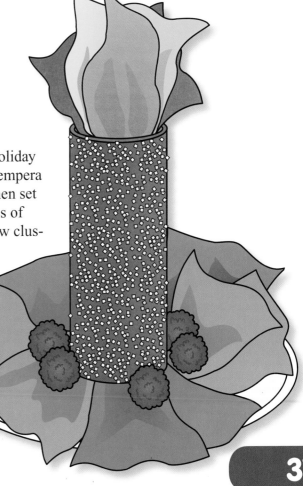

Candy Cane

Dreidel

## Shake, Rattle, and Roll!

Roll out this painting technique, and you'll have a group of grinning preschoolers on your hands! You'll also have an assortment of seasonal project possibilities. All you need is tempera paint, a golf ball, a nonbreakable transparent container with a flat bottom and a snug-fitting lid, and white construction paper cut to fit inside the container. Lay the paper inside the container, spoon about three dollops of tempera paint (same color or different colors) onto the paper, drop in the golf ball, and snap on the lid. Then grasp the container with both hands and steer the golf ball through the paint by carefully tilting, shaking, and swaying the container. When a desired effect is achieved, remove the artwork from the container and set it aside to dry. Cut the paper into a seasonal shape and add desired details.

Nancy Goldberg
B'nai Israel Schilit Nursery School
Rockville, MD

Unity Cup

Wreath

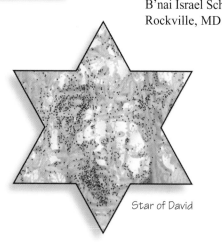

Star of David

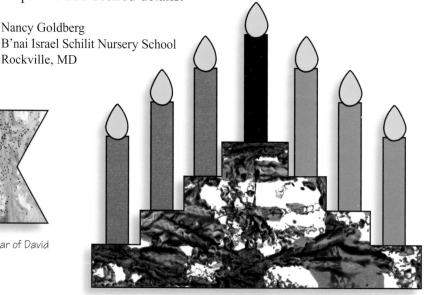

Kinara

### Leprechaun Wind Dancer

Deck the halls for St. Patrick's Day with these colorful wind dancers! Have each child glue a black construction paper band to a green leprechaun hat cutout. Then have her glue a yellow shamrock cutout to the band and help her print her name on the hat's brim. Give her six crepe paper streamer lengths—one in each color of the rainbow—to glue to the back of the hat cutout. Ahh…it's the look of the Irish!

Sarah Booth
Messiah Nursery School
South Williamsport, PA

### Pretty Rainbows

Spring rain means lots of rainbows, so color your room with these pretties. For each child, use a permanent marker to draw a rainbow on a piece of clear Con-Tact covering. Peel off the backing and then have each child tear small pieces of colored tissue paper and stick them inside the rainbow. (If desired, provide a picture of a rainbow for youngsters to use as a reference.) Once the sticky side is covered, trim off the excess as shown. To complete the project, help each child write her name on cloud cutouts and glue the cutouts to each end. Hang the rainbows from the ceiling or tape them to the windows for a suncatcher effect.

Lola M. Smith
Hilliard, OH

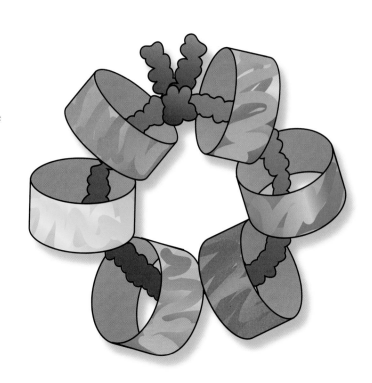

### Rainbow Bracelets

These beautiful bracelets sport the colors of the rainbow! For each child, cut six one-inch-wide loops from cardboard tubes. Have each youngster paint one loop in each of the colors of the rainbow—red, orange, yellow, green, blue, and purple. When the paint is completely dry, ask the child to string the loops (in any order she wishes) onto a pipe cleaner. Wrap the pipe cleaner around her wrist and twist the ends together to secure the bracelet. What a colorful accessory!

Betty Silkunas
Lower Gwynedd Elementary
Ambler, PA

### Waxed Paper Wreaths

Try this perfect-for-preschool approach to making wreaths and you'll be planning a wreath project for many different occasions! To make an Easter egg wreath, cut a supply of egg shapes from colorful construction paper. Next, trace onto waxed paper the outline of a paper plate and then squeeze glue along the outline. Lay the cutouts atop the glue so that they overlap slightly. Add a dot of glue between the overlapped parts, as needed, and add egg details using tempera paints and cotton swabs. When the glue and paint are dry, simply peel the wreath off the waxed paper! Punch two side-by-side holes in one shape, thread a length of raffia (or ribbon) through the holes, and tie the ends to make a bow. How precious!

Chrissy L. Rueck
PrimeTime Childhood Learning Center
Belford, NJ

## Extraordinary Eggs

These pretty-as-can-be Easter eggs are "eggs-tra" easy to make! Use a spray bottle of water to lightly mist a 12" x 18" sheet of white construction paper. Press an assortment of torn tissue paper scraps on the dampened paper, overlapping the scraps as desired. (Bright and dark colors of tissue paper yield the best results.) Then use the spray bottle to mist the tissue-covered paper. When the project is dry, remove the tissue paper and trim the colorful construction paper into an egg shape. Spread glue along the bottom of the egg and press a handful of Easter grass atop the glue. There you have it! An extraordinary egg!

Rachel Castro
Albuquerque, NM

## Excellent Eggs

The Easter bunny never had eggs like these! To prepare, purchase a class supply of Styrofoam eggs (available at craft stores). Cut colorful wrapping paper into 1" x 1" squares. Provide each child with an egg, a small paintbrush, and a cup of glue. Have her use the brush to cover the egg with glue. Then have her press wrapping paper squares onto the egg. Encourage the child to overlap the squares, cover the entire egg with paper, and then brush a thin layer of glue over the egg. Set the egg on a sheet of waxed paper to dry. To create an eye-catching display, fill a basket with Easter grass and arrange the eggs in it.

Debby Moon
School for Little People
Wichita Falls, TX

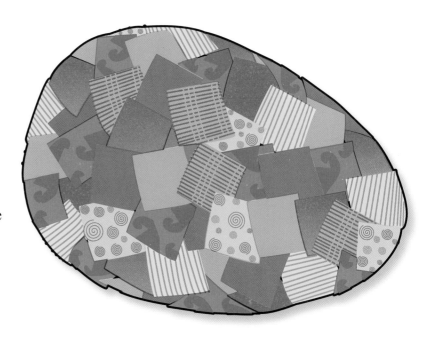

## Look What Hatched!

Feathers will be flying in your classroom when youngsters make this fun craft project. To make one chick, trace a pear shape onto a large sheet of yellow construction paper. Next use an X-acto knife to cut about 15 one-half-inch slits in the bottom part of the shape. Cut out the shape; then glue on paper eyes and a beak. Slide a yellow feather into each slot. (Feather dusters are a cheap source of feathers.) Turn the chick over; then tape each feather to the back. To really cause a hullabaloo, display these chicks together in a nest created by weaving together strips of brown paper.

Lisa Marie Bouldry
McLean Child Care Center
Belmont, MA

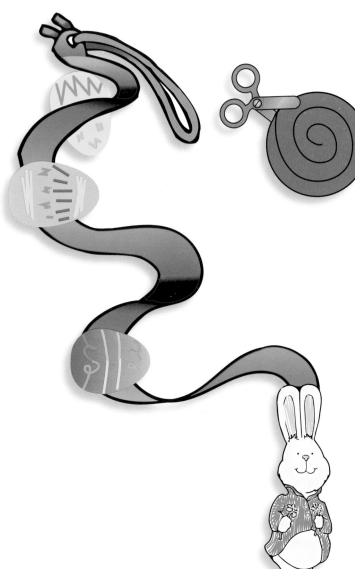

## Round and Round Rabbit

Little ones will enjoy watching this craft swirl and spin from the ceiling. To make one, cut out a large circle from construction paper. Then cut the circle into a spiral as shown. Next, invite a child to use crayons to draw designs on several construction paper eggs. Have the child glue the eggs onto the paper spiral. Next, provide the child with a copy of the rabbit pattern on page 104. Have her color the rabbit and then glue it to the end of the spiral. Punch a hole in the top of the spiral. Thread a length of ribbon through the hole and hang the spiral in your classroom. Hippity, hoppity, Easter's on its way!

Kate Buschur
Village Childcare
Kettering, OH

## Bunny Frame

This frame should be given to "some-bunny" special! To make one project, take a close-up picture of a child; then trim the photo into a circle. Mount the photo onto the center of a small paper plate. Glue white cotton balls around the photo. Glue pink cotton balls onto two poster-board bunny-ear shapes. Staple the ears to the top of the plate. Write an Easter message on a construction paper copy of the bow tie pattern on page 104; then staple the tie to the front of the plate. If desired, attach a strip of self-adhesive magnetic tape to the back of the frame. Adorable!

Diane DiMarco
Country Kids Preschool
Groton, MA

Happy Easter

### Handy Bunnies

This craft is sure to be a hands-down favorite! To make one bunny, paint a child's hand (excluding the thumb) white. Help the child separate her fingers into a V shape; then press her hand onto a sheet of construction paper. When the child's hand is clean and the paint is dry, direct the child to glue on paper eyes and a pom-pom nose. Next have her use markers to add whiskers and a smile. Have her also add pink paint to the bunny's ears. Finally, have the child twist the center of a tissue-paper rectangle and then glue it to the bunny to represent a bow tie.

Leigh Ann Clark
First Baptist Kindergarten
Eufaula, AL

### Looks Like Stained Glass!

Decorate your classroom for Easter, spring, or any other holiday or season with this simple craft. Provide each child with a piece of sturdy plastic shelf liner. Invite her to choose a color of fabric paint and then paint a design on the liner. When the paint is dry, have the child add another painted design using a different color or glitter glue. After the child has painted the liner as she desires, cut it into a seasonal shape such as an egg or a flower. Punch a hole in the top of the shape. Thread a length of ribbon through the hole and then hang the completed craft in your classroom.

Amy Drake
Westview Child Care Ministry
Fort Wayne, IN

## Flower Basket

A-tisket, a-tasket, turn a cereal box into a flower basket! To make a basket, trim the panels of a cereal box to create handles as shown. Paint the box twice with tempera paint. When the paint is dry, glue on construction paper flower shapes. Fill the basket with plastic grass and Easter goodies. These sturdy boxes hold lots of treats, so fill them well!

Suzanne Mayo
Our Lady of Peace
Fords, NJ

## Just Ducky!

Caution: Little ones could go "quackers" over this adorable duck project! To make the duck, copy the pattern from page 105 onto white construction paper. Color the bill orange and then use yellow tempera paint to sponge-paint the duck. (For a duck with texture, sponge-paint with a mixture of one part yellow tempera paint, two parts glue, and two parts nonmenthol shaving cream.) When the paint is dry, cut out the duck and tape a craft stick to the back of the cutout for support.

To make the water, fold in half a thin white paper plate. Scallop the fold line without cutting into the plate rim. Then unfold the plate, press it flat, and sponge-paint it with blue tempera paint. When the paint is dry, refold the plate, slip the duck into the water, and display the project on a tabletop. Quack, quack!

## Make Way for Ducklings!

This springtime project is a textural treat for little fingers to make. To create the scene, first use blue fingerpaint to paint a piece of paper. When the paint is dry, cut out a pond shape; then glue it onto a large piece of construction paper. Next cut cloud shapes out of white felt to glue above the pond. To make each fuzzy duck, gently pull one end of a yellow cotton ball; then twist that part of the cotton ball to represent the duck's tail. Glue the cotton ball onto the scene; then add a felt beak and eye to the cotton ball to complete the duck. After each duck has been added, use markers to add legs to the ducks and other details to the scene.

adapted from an idea by Angelia Dagnanl
Royale Childcare and Learning Center
Knoxville, TN

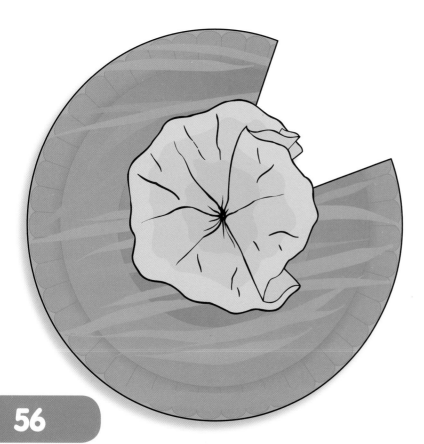

## Lily Pad Look-Alikes

Leapin' lily pads! These froggy hangouts look like the real thing! To make one, cut a triangle shape from the rim of a small, thick paper plate. Then paint the plate green. Next, use food coloring to tint a container of water red. Fold a coffee filter in half several times, dip one corner of the folded filter into the water, and then unfold the filter. When the painted plate and filter are dry, gather and twist the center of the filter and tape (or staple) it near the point where the triangle was cut out. Hey, come on over to my pad!

Nancy M. Lotzer
Farmers Branch, TX

## Turtle Love

Youngsters are sure to love making as many of these terrific turtles as their hearts desire! To make one, simply make a fist and then dip your knuckles and thumb into a shallow pan of green or brown paint. Press your knuckles and thumb onto paper. When the paint is dry, use markers or more paint to add facial features, legs, a tail, and details to the turtle's shell. Youngsters can make all types of turtles with this easy project that's tops!

Al Trautman
Milwaukee, WI

## Too Cute Turtles!

These reptiles are simply irresist-ible! To make the shell, paint one side of a nine-inch square of bubble wrap the color of your choice. Press the painted side of the wrap onto a nine-inch square of white construction paper. When the paint is dry, cut a large circular turtle shell from the paper. Next, cut out a turtle head, a tail, and four legs from construction paper. Use crayons to add desired details to the cutouts and then glue the cutouts under the rim of the shell. There you have it! A turtle that is just too cute!

Diane Muldoon
St. Matthew's Nursery School
Maple Glen, PA

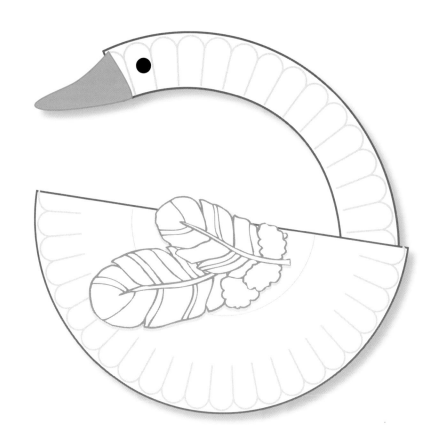

## Lovely Swans

Swim into spring with these simple swans! To make one, cut a thin white paper plate in half; then cut away the rim of the plate from one half. Glue the rim to the intact plate half, as shown, to form the swan's neck. Then glue on an orange construction paper beak and add a sticky-dot eye. Add a few pretty white craft feathers to complete this beautiful bird!

Leita Oberhofer
Newport News, VA

## Fine-Feathered Friends

These birds look so "tweet" tucked into nests of plastic grass. To make one, cut a cardboard tube into two pieces—one shorter than the other. Paint both pieces. When the paint is dry, glue the shorter piece to the longer piece as shown, clipping them together while the glue is drying. Remove the clips; then glue on feathers, wiggle eye stickers, and a paper beak. Display these birds in nests (boxes of plastic grass) tucked in quiet corners of your classroom or throughout your school.

Kimberli Carrier
Wise Owl Preschool
Nashua, NH

## A Handful of Lilies

Since the lily is a favorite flower this time of year, have your little ones make a handful to give to a special staff member or class helper. To make one lily, trace a child's hand onto white construction paper; then cut it out. Also cut out a stem and leaves from green construction paper. Wrap the hand cutout into a cone shape; then staple the leaves, stem, and flower together as shown. Bend down the fingers to resemble petals. Insert yellow pipe cleaners into the flower. Finally, twist green chenille around the stem of the flower. Wrap a piece of tissue paper around several of the flowers or insert them in a vase.

Jeri Gardner
Reid Memorial Preschool
Augusta, GA

## Tulip Time

Have youngsters make a row of tulips to brighten windowsills and shelves this spring! To make one tulip, use tempera paint to paint a cardboard tube green. For each tulip color, mix three teaspoons of water and one-half teaspoon of liquid dishwashing detergent into a cup of tempera paint. Cut one section of a Styrofoam egg carton to resemble a tulip; then paint it. When the paint is dry, glue paper leaves onto the side of the cardboard tube, glue the tulip onto the top of the tube, and glue a colored pom-pom onto the center of the tulip. Ta-da! Tulips!

Cathy McDonald
Thompson Elementary School
Jacksonville, NC

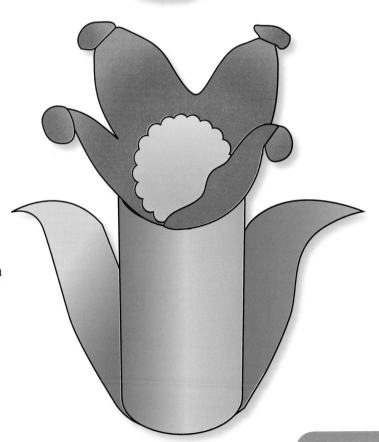

## Wishing Upon a Dandelion

When it comes to making a springtime wish, this dandelion look-alike works like a charm! To make a dandelion, dip a large gift bow into a mixture of white tempera paint and glue. Repeatedly stamp the bow onto a sheet of colored construction paper until a desired result is achieved. Then sprinkle the wet paint with iridescent glitter. Next, use a cotton swab and tempera paint to add a stem and grass. For an eye-catching display, post each child's dandelion project with her dictated wish on a bulletin board titled "Our Dandelion Wishes."

Sue Fleischmann
Waukesha County Project Head Start
Waukesha, WI

Leah's wish is for a baby sister!

## A Pretty Bouquet

Koosh balls help make pretty flowers for a springtime display! Have a child dip a small Koosh ball into one or two colors of tempera paint and then press the ball onto a sheet of construction paper. After making several flowers, allow the paint to dry. Then have the youngster use a green marker to add stems and leaves.

Donna Leonard
Dyersville Head Start
Dyersville, IA

## Floral Fabric Posies

Aren't these flowers just fabulous? To prepare to make these floral creations, cut scraps of several different floral fabrics into small pieces. Next trace a flower shape onto a sheet of white construction paper. To decorate a posy, use a paintbrush to glue the scraps over the flower shape. When the glue is dry, cut out the flower; then glue the flower to a green construction-paper stem with leaves. Display these flowers together to create a garden that will delight every eye!

Alison Link
Englewood Elementary
Port Charlotte, FL

## Pretty Posies in Pots

Start by asking each child to paint a colorful piece of construction paper using the painting tool of her choice, such as a sponge, a Ping-Pong ball, or a brush. When the paint is dry, cut each child's page into a large flower shape. Next, have each child use tempera paint to paint her own terra-cotta pot. Take a picture of each child standing in front of a brightly colored piece of bulletin board paper. Cut each child's picture into a circle; then glue the circle to the center of her flower. Laminate the flowers. Mount each flower onto an unsharpened pencil. Place a piece of green Styrofoam topped with plastic grass in each child's pot. Insert the child's pencil flower into the pot. Finally, add the message shown by sliding it into a plastic cardholder that has been added to the pot.

Martha Briggs
Rosemont Tuesday/Thursday School
Fort Worth, TX

61

### Pint-Size Piñatas

This craft contains surprise treats for students to enjoy on Cinco de Mayo (May 5). A week before this Mexican holiday, have each child make his own miniature piñata. To make one, place a small handful of wrapped candy on a paper plate. Fold the plate in half; then staple the edges of the plate together so the candy is hidden inside. Provide each child with a plate; then have him glue on tissue paper squares. When the glue is dry, invite the child to glue streamers to the straight edge of the piñata. Punch a hole in the curved edge of the piñata and then thread a length of yarn through the hole. Hang the piñatas around your room. On Cinco de Mayo, invite each child to break open his piñata and enjoy the surprises inside.

Liesl Bockelmann
Our Savior Lutheran
Austin, TX

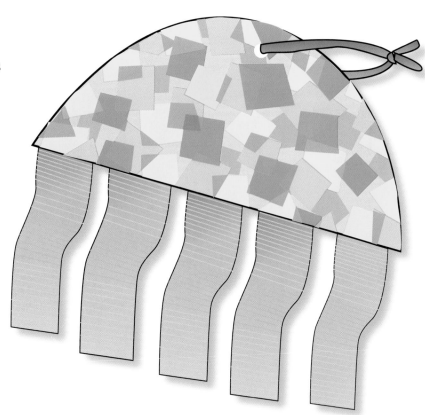

### Mother's Day Corsage

Make moms feel special with these crafty corsages. To make the flowers, cut four equal-size circles from two flattened coffee filters. Pinch each circle in the center; then dip the edges into diluted food coloring. Allow the flowers to dry; then add a stem to each one by twisting a five-inch-long piece of green pipe cleaner around the pinched center. Add leaves to each flower stem by poking the free end of the pipe cleaner through scraps of green crepe paper streamer. Then twist all four flower stems together and poke them through the center of a four-inch doily. Add a ribbon bow to complete this cute corsage!

Cheryl Cicioni
Kindernook Preschool
Lancaster, PA

## Ladybug Card

Wish moms a happy Mother's Day with the help of these lovely little ladybugs! To make a card, trace a simple ladybug shape on a half sheet of red construction paper as shown. Program the card with the text shown. Then cut a circle from red paper to match the size of the ladybug's body. Have a child make black tempera paint fingerprints over one side of the circle to resemble the ladybug's spots. Help him cut the circle in half. Then use a brad to attach the two halves over the ladybug body as shown. Have the child sign his name and take this creepy-crawly card home for Mom to read!

Peggy Miller
Rabbit Hill Nursery School
Springfield, PA

## Made With Love

You'll need to be a little crafty to successfully pull off this Mother's Day surprise! On the guise of an unrelated activity, ask each child to invite his mom (or another special woman in his life) to drop by school and make a tempera paint print of each of her hands. When the prints are dry, have each child use a different color of tempera paint to make his handprints atop those of his loved one. Also have each child sign his name to a sweet verse like the one shown. Invite him to decorate a few heart shapes too. Then cut out the pieces of each child's project, mount them on a 12" x 18" sheet of colorful construction paper, and ready the project for hanging. You can count on this special gift being a hands-down favorite for years to come!

Angie Hassan
The Learning Express Preschool
Lafayette, LA

### Pretty Polka-Dotted Ladies

Youngsters will scurry over to make one of these ladybugs. To make one, cut a pair of same-size circles from waxed paper. Place one of the circles, waxed side up, on a newspaper-covered surface. Sprinkle red crayon shavings over the circle; then add black construction-paper circles and antennae. Place the remaining circle on top of the first. Cover the layers with a second piece of newspaper; then use an iron (on a low heat setting) to melt the wax. Are you seeing spots yet?

Kimberli Carrier
Wise Owl Preschool
Nashua, NH

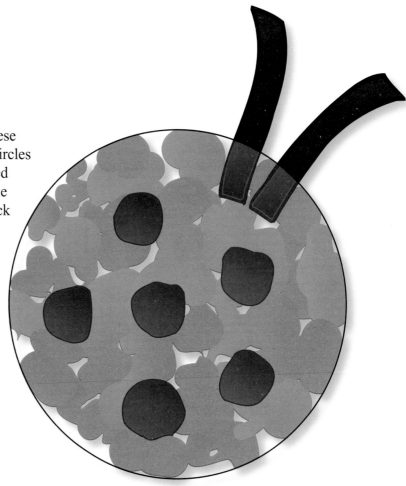

### Lovable Ladybug Rocks

Your students will go buggy for these ladybug rock keepsakes! To prepare, gather a class supply of small, smooth stones. Have each child paint a stone with red acrylic paint. When the paint is dry, direct the child to use a black permanent marker to add details such as eyes, a shell dividing line, and spots. Have students take these cute critters home to share with their families.

Jeni Van Buer
Prince of Peace Academy
Clinton, IA

## Cute-As-a-Button Bug

Have you ever seen such a cute bug? In advance, use a knitting needle (or another straight and pointed object) to poke holes in opposite sides of individual paper towel tubes (for the wings). To make a bug, a child uses crayons to decorate a vertical half sheet of copy paper to her liking. Assist her in gluing the paper to the outside of the tube. Then use the knitting needle to reopen the previously made holes and to thread a plastic newspaper bag through the openings. Trim the resulting wings to a desired length. For the head, cut out a construction paper oval with a tab (see the illustration). Hole-punch the top of the oval and then assist the child in threading a pipe cleaner length through the hole and twisting and shaping it into antennae. Also help the child add facial features from available craft supplies. Last, glue the tab inside the cardboard tube. This cutie-pie critter is ready to take flight!

Eileen Mattas
Little Learners Preschool
Glenview, IL

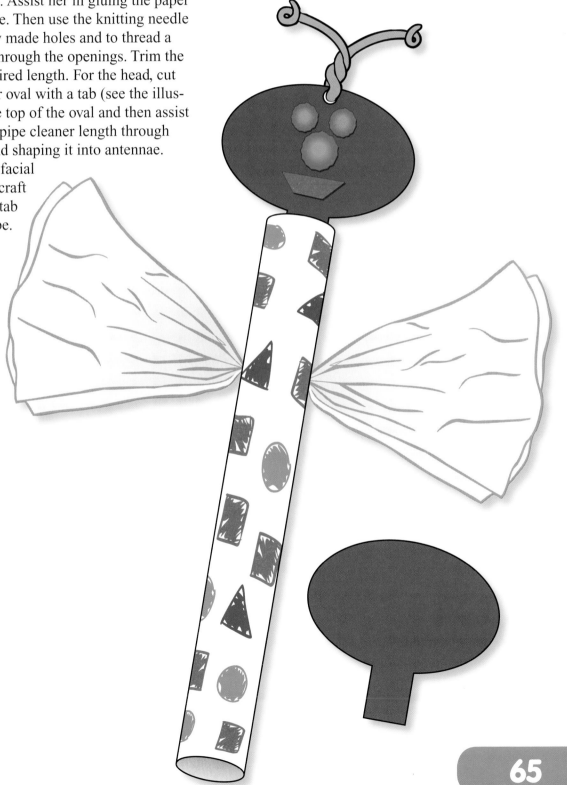

## Circles and Caterpillars

Invite youngsters to wiggle right over to an art center to print these circular creepy crawlers. To prepare, pour each different color of paint into a separate shallow container. Provide a number of different circular items for students to print with, such as film containers, plastic spools, and plastic cups. Provide each child with a length of white construction paper. Direct him to use the objects to print a caterpillar onto his paper. Then have him use a fork to print grass. When the paint is dry, have him add sticky-dot eyes and marker details. These art prints also spark counting conversations. "How many circles long is your caterpillar? How many circles are red?" Cool!

Janet Polizois
Play'n Learn Childcare
Flanders, NJ

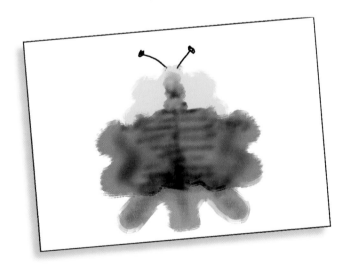

## A Pretty Butterflies

Have your preschoolers flutter on over to the art table to make these easy butterfly paintings! To make one, fold a 12" x 18" sheet of white construction paper in half. Open the paper; then have the child choose two to four different colors of tempera paint. Spoon a bit of each color onto the fold of the paper. Refold the paper; then have the child press from the fold outward to spread the paint. Open the paper and allow the paint to dry. Then use a marker to add features. There you have it, a one-of-a-kind butterfly!

Jackie Grasso
Good Shepherd Episcopal School
Friendswood, TX

## Honey of a Bee

"Bee-ware"! This cute-as-a-button bee may create quite a buzz in your classroom! To make the body, use yellow tempera paint to cover the bottom of a small, thick paper plate. When the paint dries, paint stripes using black tempera paint. For the wings, flatten two coffee filters. To make the bee's head, add facial features to a yellow construction paper circle. Then, to make antennae, tape the middle of a V-shaped piece of black pipe cleaner to the back of the head. Glue the wings and head to the body and this honey of a bee is ready to take flight!

Julie Gimmel
Quantico Child Development Center
Quantico, VA

## Ant Antics

That's a busy ant! To make an ant trail, lay a sheet of white construction paper in the bottom of a rectangular pan. Use tongs to submerge a Ping-Pong ball in brown tempera paint. Drop the paint-coated ball on the paper. Then grasp opposite sides of the pan, lift the pan, and tilt it back and forth, making the Ping-Pong ball roll. Recoat the Ping-Pong ball and repeat the process one or two times until a desired effect is achieved. Then remove the artwork from the pan and set it aside to dry. To make an ant, glue three pom-poms side by side on the paper and draw six tiny ant legs extending from the middle pom-pom. Be sure to remind little ones that real ants are fun to watch but should never be touched.

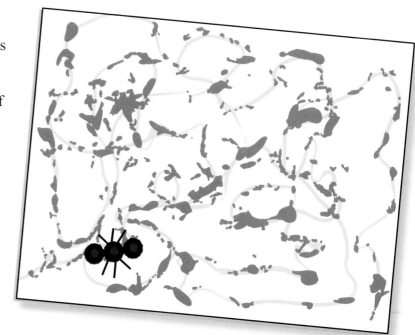

Melinda Blackwill
Hays, KS

## Dandy Dragonflies

These bugs are big, blue, and beautiful! For each child, gather four thin white paper plates—three small and one large. Have each child paint the back of each plate with blue tempera paint. When the paint is dry, staple the four plates together, as shown, to form a dragonfly. Glue on two large eyes cut from white and black construction paper scraps. To make wings, tie a knot in the center of an 8" x 15" piece of white tulle netting; then hot-glue the knot to the dragonfly's body. Hang the finished dragonflies from your classroom ceiling.

Shelley Williams
Children's College
Layton, UT

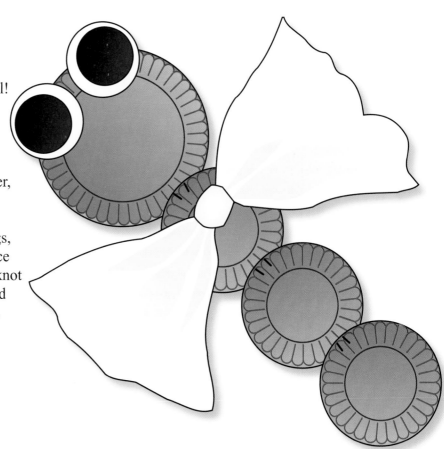

## Dragonfly Magnet

To make this dazzling dragonfly, cut out a pair of wings from laminating film. Use glitter glue or glitter paint to decorate the wings; then glue them onto a colorful jumbo craft stick. Attach a self-adhesive magnetic strip to the back of the stick. Add wiggle eye stickers and the dragonfly is ready to take flight!

Diana Shepard
First Presbyterian Preschool
Wilmington, NC

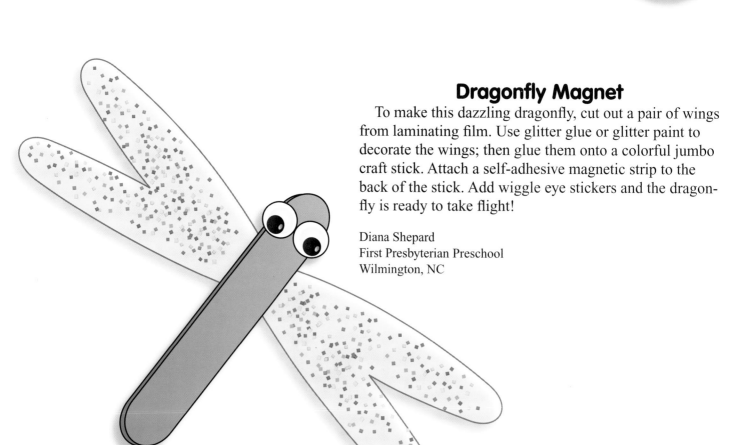

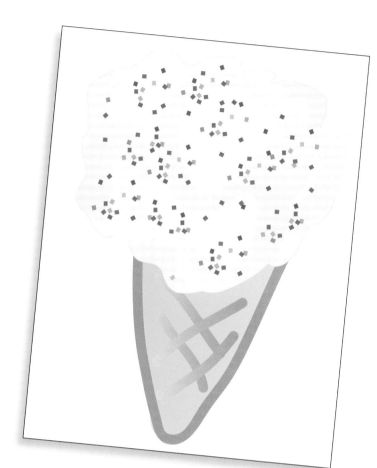

## Here's the Scoop

Briskly fold two parts nonmenthol shaving cream with one part white glue. Add food coloring, if desired. When the mixture is slightly stiff and shiny, get ready for a "scooper-duper" art activity! On a large sheet of construction paper, draw an ice-cream cone. Drop a dollop of the mixture onto the paper above the cone and then spread it around with a craft stick until it resembles a scoop of ice cream. While the mixture is wet, sprinkle on some glitter.

Debbie Clark
Little Red Caboose Preschool
Virden, IL

## Garden Stones

These stepping-stones make precious gifts any time of the year! To prepare, collect a class supply of empty frozen-entree plates (without dividers). Next, mix quick-setting concrete (such as Quikrete) in a large mixing bucket away from the children. Follow the package directions to prepare enough thick pastelike mixture to fill an entree plate for each child. Put a small amount of the concrete in a separate plate for each child. Direct each child to put a hand in his dish to make an impression. When the concrete has hardened, remove each stone from its plastic dish. Finally, decoratively wrap each stone and attach the poem shown.

Donna Pollhammer
YMCA Chipmunk Preschool
Westminster, MD

My hands were once so tiny.
I needed so much care.
Thank you so much, Daddy,
For always being there!

## A Holder and a Hug, Too

Dad is sure to find this gift amusing and handy! To make one pencil holder, cut a piece of construction paper to match the height and circumference of a plastic container (such as a powdered-drink container). Label the center of the paper with the child's name. Add a picture of the child. Next trace the child's hands and feet onto construction paper. Cut out the hand and foot shapes along with a 1" x 11" strip of construction paper that is the same color as the hand cutouts. If desired, laminate all of the pieces.

To assemble the gift, use tape to secure the labeled paper around the container. Use an X-acto knife to cut a vertical 1¹/₂" slit on opposite sides of the container. Slide the construction-paper strip into the slits so that it is extended; then slide the center of the strip into the container so that it folds inside the can. Glue one hand cutout to each end of the strip and the feet cutouts to the bottom of the container. Give Dad the holder to fill with pens and pencils. Then, when he needs a hug, he can just give the hands a tug!

Carol L. Hammill
Community Christian Preschool
Fountain Valley, CA

## Watercolor Sunset

There's nothing like a spectacular sunset at the beach! Invite each of your preschoolers to make her own version of this summer scene with watercolor paints. First, have her use a spray bottle to dampen a sheet of white construction paper with water. Then have her use watercolors to paint bands of colors across the paper. Hold the paper by the top corners over a tray, allowing the paint to drip and the colors to blend together. When the paint is dry, have the child glue a half circle cut from bright orange paper near the bottom of the scene. Finally, help her glue on a torn strip of blue paper to simulate the ocean's waves. Beautiful!

Nancy O'Toole
Ready Set Grow
Grand Rapids, MN

## Beach Props

Is there a beach in your classroom at this time of year? Enhance children's imaginary play by making simple sunglasses from craft foam! Use the sunglasses patterns on page 106 to make tagboard tracers. Then use the tracers to create craft foam glasses. Punch holes in the top corners of the glasses. Then twist a length of pipe cleaner through each hole to create an earpiece. Glue colored cellophane over the eyeholes to make the glasses more realistic. Invite each child to choose a pair of glasses and then decorate them with slick or puffy fabric paint. They'll look just "beach-y"!

Nancy Wolfgram
Kindercare Learning Center #1111
Lincoln, NE

## A Seaside Pail

Your youngsters will really dig this beach-themed art project! Gather the materials listed below; then help each child follow the directions. Once the pails are finished, display them with a shovel cutout on a bulletin board titled "We Dig Preschool!"

**Materials needed for one pail:**
light blue construction paper pail shape
   (approximately $7\frac{1}{2}$" x 10")
1" x 12" construction paper strip
tan crayon
shallow pans, each containing a thin
   layer of paint
sea creature–shaped sponges
marker
stapler

**Directions:**
1. Use a tan crayon to color the bottom of the pail to resemble sand.
2. Fold the pail in half lengthwise; then unfold it.
3. Dip a shaped sponge in paint and then make a print on one half of the pail. Repeat with a second sponge on the same half of the pail cutout.
4. Fold the pail, and use your hand to smooth over the paper's surface to transfer the paint print to the opposite side. Unfold the pail.
5. After the paint is dry, use a marker to draw facial features on each sea creature.
6. Staple a paper strip to each side of the pail top to make a handle.

Judy Kelley
Lilja School
Natick, MA

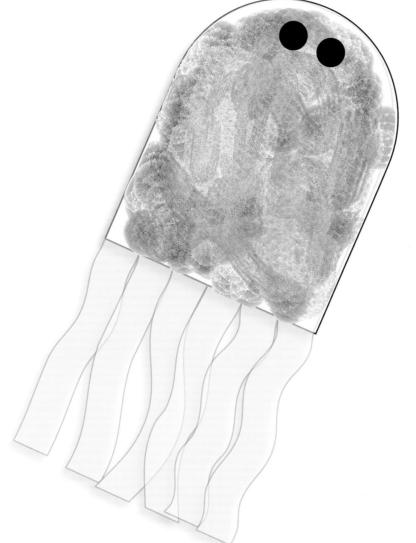

## Just-Right Jellyfish

Need a simple summer craft for your pre-schoolers? This jellyfish is just the thing! To make one, cut out a tagboard jellyfish body similar to the one shown. Then cut a piece of waxed paper so that it fits the top of the tagboard and hangs several inches below it. Have a child paint the tagboard. When the paint is dry, direct the child to glue the waxed paper over the tagboard and then cut the bottom of the paper into strips to create tentacles. Have the child add two sticky-dot eyes and the jellyfish is complete!

Sue Millard
Playhouse Nursery School
Maple Grove, MN

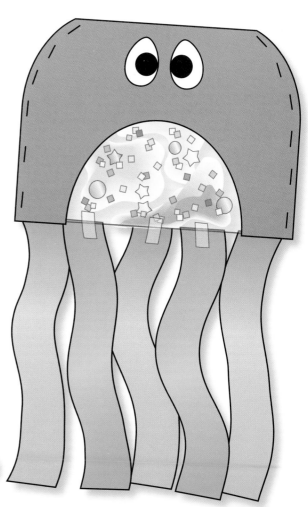

## "Gel-lyfish"

This peekaboo project is perfect to enhance a study of ocean critters! For each child, fold a sheet of construction paper in half. Draw three curved lines as shown. Have the child cut along the lines and discard the scraps. Then ask her to draw two eyes above the center cutout. Next, help her squirt a bit of clear hair gel into a zippered plastic bag. Then have her sprinkle in some glitter and metallic confetti. Squeeze out any air and seal the plastic bag. Tape the bag inside the jellyfish cutout so that the seal is covered by the paper. Then staple around the edges of the paper. Finally, have the child tape a few lengths of crepe paper streamer to the bottom of the jellyfish to create tentacles.

Karen Reed
Trailside Daycare
East Providence, RI

### Handprint Crabs

To make a crab, a child dips her hands into washable red tempera paint. Then she presses them onto a sheet of construction paper so that the palm prints overlap and the fingerprints extend in opposite directions. When the paint is dry, she draws on a smile, then attaches a sticky-dot eye on each thumbprint. Finally, she glues sand underneath the crab to complete the picture. These cute crustaceans can't be beat!

Kimberly Calhoun
Tutor Time Learning Center
Apex, NC

### Paper Plate Crabs

To make one, paint the back of a paper plate orange. When the paint is dry, fold the plate in half and staple the edges together. Glue on a pair of black pom-pom eyes and construction paper claws and legs. Quick and cute!

Nicole Petro
Wee Vikes Learning Center
Glen Gardner, NJ

## Paper Bag Octopus

What has eight arms and is a cute craft? A paper bag octopus, of course! To make one, paint a small paper lunch bag with purple tempera paint. When the paint is dry, stuff some tissue paper into the bottom and then use ribbon or string to tie the bag closed above the stuffed section. Cut the remainder of the bag into eight strips; then twist each one to form an arm. Flip the bag over and add two sticky-dot eyes and a sweet smile to what is now the octopus's head. What a friendly ocean critter!

Crystal Hampton
Kare Nursery
Arcadia, CA

## "Sense-ational" Starfish

This craft uses a fabulous textured paint with lots of sensory appeal! To prepare, mix several different colors of puff paint. For each color, combine two tablespoons of washable tempera paint and $\frac{1}{3}$ cup of white glue. Fold in two cups of nonmentholated shaving cream until the color is well blended. (For best results, use the paint soon after mixing it.)

To make one starfish, fingerpaint a star-shaped tagboard cutout with several colors of the puff paint. Sprinkle glitter over the wet paint; then set the starfish aside to dry overnight. Youngsters will enjoy smelling, touching, and seeing this interesting paint—even when it's dry!

Beverly Folena
Creative Kids Preschool
Placerville, CA

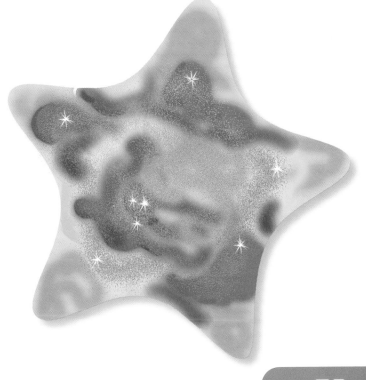

## Catch of the Day

Add a little underwater art to your classroom with these crafty fish. To prepare to make one, use a craft knife to cut slits in a clear plastic cup as shown. Then cut out construction paper fins, eyes, and a tail. Have a child use glitter glue to decorate the fins and tail. When the glue is dry, direct the child to slip the fins into the slits and glue the tail to the bottom of the cup. Have the child glue an eye onto each side of the cup and then stuff the cup with a sheet of colorful tissue paper.

To display these fine fish, punch a small hole in each cup and thread a length of yarn through the hole. Tie a large knot in the bottom of the yarn and then hang the fish in your classroom. Caught a big one!

Barbara Fishel
Owl Hill Learning Center
Lititz, PA

## Sparkly Fish

Wait 'til you "sea" these fanciful fish! To make one, cut a simple fish shape from brightly colored construction paper; then cut out the center portion as shown. Next, squirt some glitter glue onto the center of a piece of waxed paper slightly larger than the fish shape. Use a paintbrush to spread the glue with short strokes, making the design resemble fish scales. When the glue is dry, trim the waxed paper and then glue or tape it behind the opening in the fish cutout. Add a dot eye and a friendly fishy smile, and this project is ready to display!

Barb Stefaniuk
Kerrobert Tiny Tots Playschool
Kerrobert, Saskatchewan, Canada

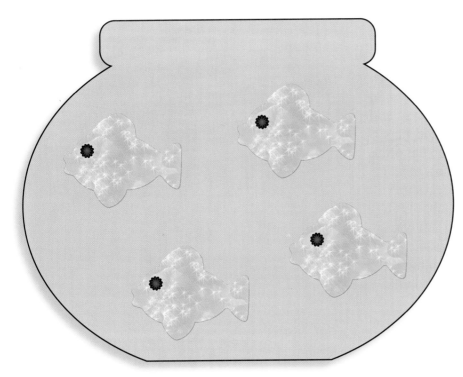

### Glittery Goldfish

From a distance, these sparkly swimmers look real! Mix together white glue and tempera paint—one part to three parts, respectively. Use the mixture to fingerpaint directly onto a nine-inch length of foil. Then sprinkle the painted foil with iridescent glitter. When the foil is dry, lay a goldfish cutout (pattern on page 107) on the unpainted side of the foil and trace around it. Cut out the shape, flip it over, and add a pom-pom eye. For an eye-catching display, showcase the glittery goldfish inside a giant fish bowl cutout. Wow! Those fish look real!

adapted from an idea by Alma L. Flores
Imperial Valley College Development Preschool
Imperial, CA

### Blast Off!

Count down to creativity by having youngsters make these cool rockets! To prepare to make one, cut a 6½-inch half circle from tagboard; then tape the half circle into a cone shape. Use packaging or masking tape to attach the cone over the bottom of a Pringles potato chip canister as shown. Next, help a child cover the container and cone with aluminum foil. Then invite him to decorate his rocket with space-themed stickers and strips of red, white, and blue construction paper. To create engine fire for the rocket, have the child squirt some glue on the inside edge of the canister's open end; then direct him to insert pieces of red, orange, and yellow tissue paper into the opening. Hang these roaring rockets around your room for a stellar display!

Bonne Boodman
Congregation Mishkan Tefila Nursery School
Chestnut Hill, MA

## Magic Flags

There'll be stars, stripes, and surprises when you help youngsters create these American flags! To prepare, cut a 6" x 10" rectangle of white construction paper for each child; then fold back about two inches on one short side of each paper. Using a white crayon, draw a rectangle in the upper left corner of each flag-to-be; then add stars. Next, use waxed paper to mask the area inside the white rectangle you drew. Then invite a child to use a mini paint roller to paint seven red stripes over the rest of the rectangle. When the red paint is dry, have the child remove the waxed paper and color the upper left corner with a blue bingo marker. The stars will magically appear! When the blue bingo marker is dry, wrap the folded edge of the paper around a drinking straw and glue it in place. Then watch those flags wave!

Donna Pollhammer
YMCA Chipmunk Preschool
Westminster, MD

## Patriotic Prints

Here's a handy way to show allegiance during the Fourth of July. Use this idea to make a magnet, to decorate a T-shirt, or to trim a bulletin board.

**Materials needed per child:**
red, white, and blue paint (fabric paint if decorating a T-shirt)
cream-colored paper or T-shirt
silver glitter glue (or metallic fabric paint if decorating a T-shirt)
self-adhesive magnetic tape (if making a magnet)
scissors (for magnet or bulletin board trim)
paintbrush

**Directions:**
1. Paint the thumb, middle finger, and pinky finger of one hand red.
2. Paint the index and ring fingers white.
3. Paint the palm blue.
4. Press the hand on paper or fabric to make a print.
5. After the paint dries, dot on silver glitter to resemble stars.
6. Trim around the handprint (if making a magnet or trim).
7. Stick a piece of magnetic tape to the back (if making a magnet).

Jennifer Bragg
Sunset Heights
Nashua, NH

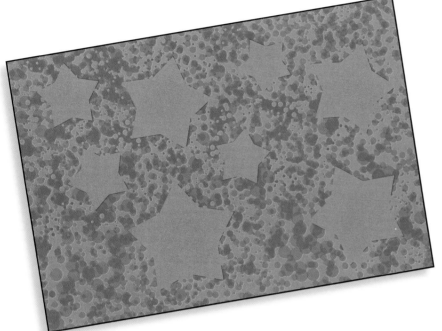

## Patriotic Painting

Celebrate Independence Day with these star-spangled paintings! Have a child lay several plastic glow-in-the-dark stars (available at craft stores) on a sheet of red, white, or blue construction paper. Then have him dip an old toothbrush into liquid watercolor or diluted tempera paint in a different patriotic shade. Direct him to hold the toothbrush over the paper and run his thumb over the bristles to make the paint "spray" onto the paper and stars. Allow the paint to dry; then lift off the stars. Negative space—neat!

Lori Alisa Burrow
Our Town Playschool
Yuba City, CA

## Fun Firecrackers

Here's a fun Fourth of July craft that makes use of excess laminating film and small cardboard tubes. In advance, save the excess film from laminated projects and cut it into strips. Also collect a class supply of small cardboard tubes. To make one firecracker, paint a cardboard tube red, white, or blue; then set it aside to dry. Use glitter glue pens to draw designs on three strips of laminating film. When the glitter is dry, staple each strip inside the tube as shown. Then glue a construction paper star to the end of each strip. Wow! Just look at those fireworks!

Debbie Bever
Harrisville Elementary
Harrisville, WV

### Fabulous Fireworks

Your youngsters will love this unique painting project! Provide a child with a large sheet of white paper. Next, have her squirt a small drop of liquid tempera paint onto the paper and then cover the paint with a margarine-tub lid. Have the child disperse the paint by hitting the center of the lid with a wooden mallet or block. To create more colorful fireworks, invite the child to squirt a different color of paint over the first color and repeat the procedure. Help the child sprinkle glitter over her completed fireworks and then set the painting aside to dry.

Marsha Feffer
Bentley Early Childhood Center
Salem, MA

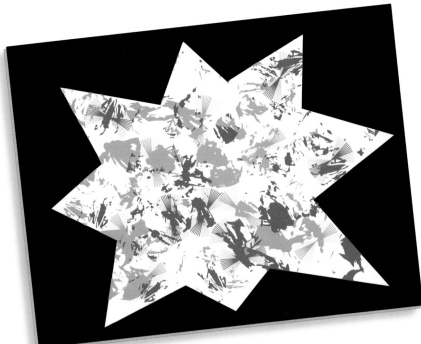

### Flashy Fireworks

This Fourth of July painting project is sure to go over with a bang! Squeeze assorted colors of tempera paint onto individual paper plates and provide a clean bottle brush for each paint color. To paint fireworks, dip the tip of a bottle brush into a paint color. Randomly dab the paint onto white construction paper with gentle twists of the brush. Repeat the process with one or more paint colors until a desired effect is achieved. Then sprinkle the wet paint with glitter and set the project aside to dry. For an eye-catching display, trim the projects into shapes that resemble exploding fireworks and post the cutouts on a backdrop of black paper.

adapted from an idea by Ann Bates
West Yadkin Head Start
Hamptonville, NC

Kirsten  Jackson  Ben

Theo  Matt  Nicholas  Shaina

Erin  Sammy  Breyanna  Beth

## Happy Birthday, William!

## Cupcake Greetings

Is today someone's special day? Ask the class to help you decorate a giant cupcake for the birthday boy or girl! From large pieces of construction paper, cut two parts of a cupcake as shown. Glue the parts together; then add a message. Ask each child to add his name and thumbprint to the cupcake top. Leave the cupcake in your art center through the day so that children can glue on colorful glitter, small paper shapes, or confetti pieces.

## I'm a Preschool Artist!

Making a personalized paint smock will have each of your preschoolers feeling like Picasso! In advance, obtain an adult-sized white T-shirt for each child. Slip a piece of cardboard inside the shirt to prevent paint from bleeding through it. Use black fabric paint to outline an artist's palette on the front of each shirt; then write "Preschool Artist" on the shirt. Set the shirt aside to dry; then cut a few small potatoes in half. When the paint is dry, work with one child at a time to make colorful fabric-paint potato prints on the palette. Keep the completed smocks in your classroom for each artist to wear when creating a masterpiece.

Ada Goren
Winston-Salem, NC

Preschool Artist

## Hats Off!

Invite your preschoolers to make these nifty hats for their noggins! To make one, cut a 20-inch circle out of white bulletin board paper. Invite a child to sponge-print a design onto the paper. When the paint is dry, hold the paper (painted side up) on the child's head. Then mold the paper to fit the child's head by wrapping colored masking tape around the paper and the child's head. Roll up the ends of the paper to create a brim for the hat. Simple to make and your preschoolers will love it! Try to top that!

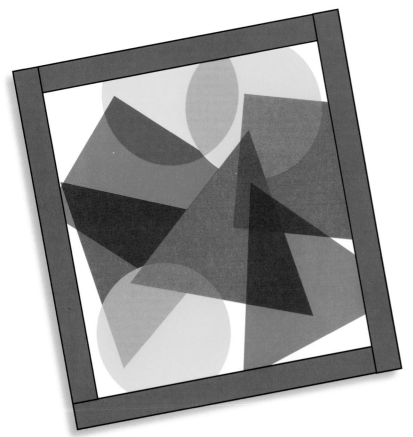

## Stained Glass Windows

Looking for a craft to help youngsters learn about colors, color mixing, and shapes? Try this sticky version of stained glass! To make one stained glass window, use loops of tape to attach a square piece of clear Con-Tact paper to a tabletop (adhesive side up). Provide a child with several shapes cut from red, yellow, and blue cellophane. Have her stick the shapes onto the Con-Tact paper to make a collage, overlapping the shapes as desired. Seal her finished collage by covering it with a sheet of clear Con-Tact paper. To create a frame for the window, staple strips of construction paper (in the child's choice of color) to the four edges. Then hang these see-through creations in a sunny window.

Sherry Gish
Highland Plaza United Methodist
 Preschool and Kindergarten
Hixon, TN

## The Art Express

To encourage a trainload of creative expression, choo-choo-choose a desired art experience. Have each youngster try the chosen technique on a 9" x 12" sheet of art paper. (For your convenience, three suggestions are provided to the right.) When the projects are dry, add paper wheels and a hitch to each one. Then display the art-related cargo behind a train engine cutout labeled "The Art Express." Each time youngsters try a new art technique, add the cargo to the train or use it to replace the cargo that's currently on display. Either way you'll have a first-class display of student-rendered artwork!

Jane FitzSimmons-Thomez
St. Mary's Preschool
Owatonna, MN

**Possible Art Experiences**

- **Plastic wrap:** Randomly drip colorful tempera paint onto art paper. Cover the art paper with plastic wrap. Touching only the plastic, smooth, smear, and swirl the paint colors.

- **Cardboard tubes:** Dip one end of a cardboard tube into a shallow container of paint and then randomly stamp the painted end onto art paper. Repeat as many times as desired.

- **Toy vehicles:** Roll a toy vehicle through a shallow container of paint and then onto art paper. Repeat as many times as desired.

### Chalk and Water Art

Here's an anytime art experience your pre-schoolers will love! First, fill a sink or large container with water. Have each child use a handheld pencil sharpener to sharpen sticks of colorful chalk into the water. Do not mix the chalk into the water—allow the chalkdust to float. You'll be able to see a swirling design form. Next, have a child lay a sheet of white construction paper on top of the water and press down very gently. Have him lift the paper off the water's surface and lay it design side up to dry. After the paper is dry, have him cut out a desired seasonal shape.

Debbie Rowland

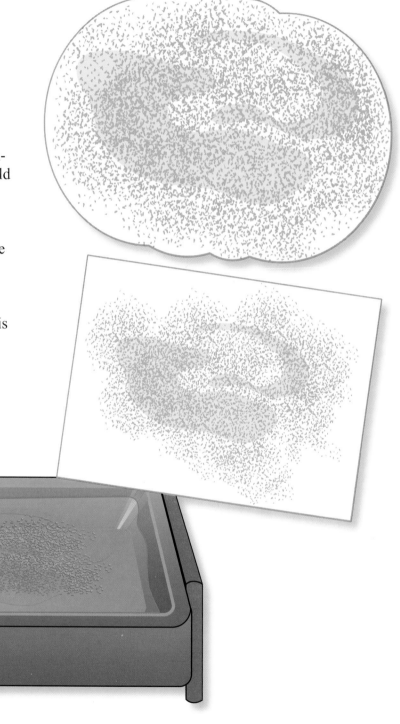

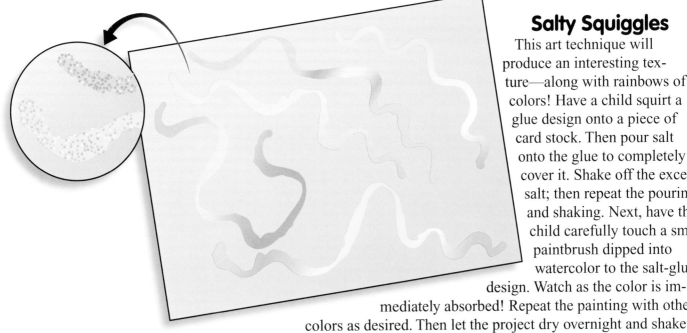

## Salty Squiggles

This art technique will produce an interesting texture—along with rainbows of colors! Have a child squirt a glue design onto a piece of card stock. Then pour salt onto the glue to completely cover it. Shake off the excess salt; then repeat the pouring and shaking. Next, have the child carefully touch a small paintbrush dipped into watercolor to the salt-glue design. Watch as the color is immediately absorbed! Repeat the painting with other colors as desired. Then let the project dry overnight and shake off any remaining salt. As a variation, have a child run the glue over the traced letters of his name, a shape, or a number.

Terri Vrasich
Noah's Ark Preschool
McHenry, IL

## Paper Cup Printing

Focus on circles with this well-rounded painting project! First, set out a few different colors of tempera paint in shallow containers. Provide a supply of drinking cups and white construction paper. Have each youngster dip the rim of a paper cup into the paint color of her choice and then print it onto her paper. Have her continue with other colors, overlapping the circles as she desires. When the paint is dry, invite her to use crayons or markers to color in the areas created by overlapping circles. Then help her cut around the perimeter of her design and glue it onto a sheet of black construction paper for a dazzling work of art!

Carrie Lacher
Friday Harbor, WA

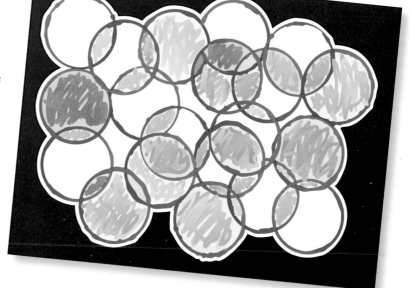

## Up, Up, and Away

Little ones take to the skies during this uplifting art experience! Use two rubber bands to mold a large bone-shaped sponge into the shape of a hot-air balloon (see below). Dip the sponge into a shallow container of tempera paint and then press it near the top of a 12" x 18" sheet of light blue construction paper. When the paint is dry, add details and scenery! What a view!

Susan Burbridge
All Saints Lutheran Preschool
Albuquerque, NM

## Feathered Shakers

Make these shakers and you'll have rhythm instruments to shake throughout the year. Cover one end of a cardboard tube with strips of masking tape. Then tape a tongue depressor onto the tube. (Craft sticks may break with heavy shaking.) Put a spoonful of beans into the tube; then use masking tape to completely cover the open end. To decorate the shaker, paint a thin layer of glue onto the tube; then cover it with tissue paper pieces and feathers. If necessary, add more glue as you apply layers. When the glue is dry, give the shaker a try. You've got rhythm!

Kathy Myles
Hicksville Nursery School
Hicksville, NY

## Slithering Snakes!

These colorful reptiles make great craft projects anytime! To make one, use bingo markers to paint different-colored circles on both sides of a paper plate. Starting along the outside rim of the plate, cut a spiral, leaving an oval shape at the center of the plate for the snake's head. Glue construction paper eyes onto the snake. Punch a hole at either tip of the snake; then tie on a length of string for hanging from the ceiling.

Christa J. Koch
Wesley Circle of Friends
Bethlehem, PA

## Buzz Around Bugs

Studying shapes? Start with circles and make these friendly and colorful circle bugs! To make a bug, each child needs four different sizes of colorful construction paper circles: two of the smallest size for the bug's eyes, one of the next larger size for the bug's head, two of the next larger size for the bug's midsection, and two of the largest circles for the bug's wings. Each child also needs two small dot stickers and crayons. Have each child assemble a bug by gluing the circles together as shown, folding the two largest circles in half before gluing them in place for wings. Have her complete the bug by putting the dot stickers on the eyes and coloring details on the bug's wings and body. Look at that colorful bug! How many circles can you find?

Niki Huff
Stilwell United Methodist Preschool
Stilwell, KS

## Dino Puppet

To make one dinosaur puppet, fold a paper plate in half and then glue the halves together. Repeatedly cut triangular shapes from around the rim area. Next embellish the dinosaur with markers, bingo markers, paint, stickers, and other craft supplies. Finally, glue halves of craft sticks to the straight edge of the plate for legs. Personalize the back of each project with a dinosaur name based on the artist's name. Look, guys! It's the gentle, plant-eating giant, Jacobosaurus!

Janie Rabb
Alphabet Alley Learning Center
Llano, TX

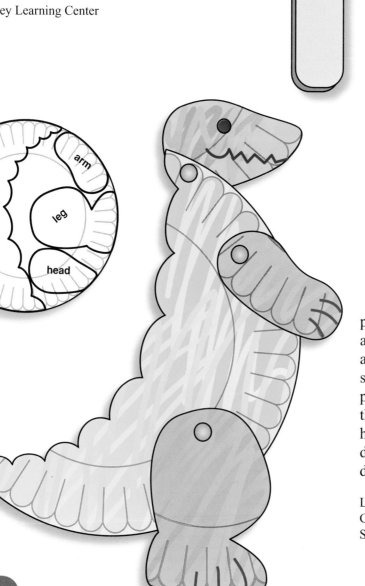

## Dynamite Dinos

These paper-plate projects make for prehistoric preschool fun! In advance, use a black marker to draw the body parts of a dinosaur on a thin white paper plate as shown. To make a dinosaur, cut out the pieces. Attach the head, arm, and leg to the dinosaur body with metal brads. Then have the child use crayons or markers to decorate the dino as desired. Will your dinosaur be fierce or friendly?

Lisa Scaglione
Children's Village Preschool
Sherrill's Ford, NC

## Beautiful Bovine

To make a cow, paint black spots on a large paper plate. Paint one small paper plate pink and another yellow. When the paint is dry, staple the pink plate near the bottom of the large plate to make a nose. Use a black marker to draw eyes, nostrils, and a mouth on the two plates. Cut the yellow plate in half; then trim the pieces to resemble horns. Staple the horns to the top back of the cow's head. Staple black construction-paper ears to the front of the plate; then bend them forward.

Pam Selby
Walls Elementary
Walls, MS

## Piggy Bank Bottles

These pink porkers are precious! To make one, glue pink construction paper around a clean plastic soda bottle with a cap. Use tacky glue to attach four legs made from empty thread spools or egg-carton cups. Curl a pink pipe cleaner by twisting it around a pencil and then sliding it off. Poke a hole in the bottom of the soda bottle and stick one end of the curly tail inside, securing it with a bit of tacky glue. Cut two triangle ears from pink construction paper. Pinch each ear in the middle and glue it in place as shown. Attach two sticky-dot eyes. Finish the bank by cutting a slit through the paper and the bottle (a teacher's job). This little piggy is ready to save!

Cheri Anderson
First Presbyterian Church Day School
DeLand, FL

## Fingerpaint Piggies

No two piggies in this precious bunch are exactly alike! To make a piggy, use your fingers to spread pink tempera paint over the entire surface of a sheet of fingerpaint paper. When the paint is dry, trace three different-size circle tracers on the paper to make a body, a head, and a snout of a pig. (Provide a variety of tracer sizes from which students can choose.) Cut out each circle; then, from your scraps, cut out two pig ears and two pig hooves. Assemble the pig as shown. Use a cotton swab and a black ink pad to add facial details. Last, curl a six-inch length of pipe cleaner to form a tail. Tape one end of the tail to the back of the project. Oink, oink!

Hollie Parker
First Presbyterian Preschool
Dunedin, FL

## Western Wear

Yahoo! Your little ones are sure to have a rootin'-tootin' good time making these cowpoke hats. Make a tagboard hat using the pattern on page 108 for each child. Direct each child to use markers to color his hat. Then cut out the hat as indicated on the pattern. Invite each child to embellish his hat with feathers, if desired. To complete the hat, staple a sentence-strip headband to fit the child's head. Then staple the hat onto the band as shown so that the narrow strips at the bottom of the hat are toward the back of the headband. How about those hats!

Carol Pochert
ABC Kids Care
Grafton, WI

## Giddyup!

Nothing's more valuable to a cowpoke than her own horse! Before youngsters make these horses, trace the pattern on page 109 onto tagboard and cut the pattern out to make a tracer. To make one horse, trace the pattern onto one side of a large, folded piece of brown kraft paper. Cut along the outline through both thicknesses. Attach lengths of yarn to a masking-tape strip; then attach the strip to one of the horse shapes for the mane. Glue the shapes together along the edges, leaving the bottom of the neck open and making sure that the yarn is on the outside. Use markers to add details to both sides of the horse shape. Slide a wrapping-paper roll into the neck opening; then glue it closed. Finally, attach a length of yarn to the horse for a rein. Ride 'em, cowpoke!

Carol Pochert

### Open Wide!

To make one alligator, tear green paper to make the alligator's long body. Next, tear another long piece for the tail and then glue it to the body. Continue tearing pieces and gluing them together until the alligator has jaws and legs. Add torn white and black paper eyes. Don't forget to give the alligator lots of sharp, white teeth! Display the alligators on a swamp scene made with blue plastic wrap and torn paper trees and plants.

Julie Shields
Brookeland School
Brookeland, TX

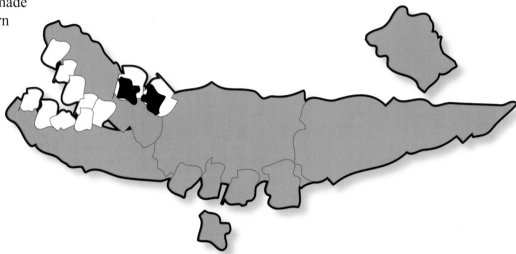

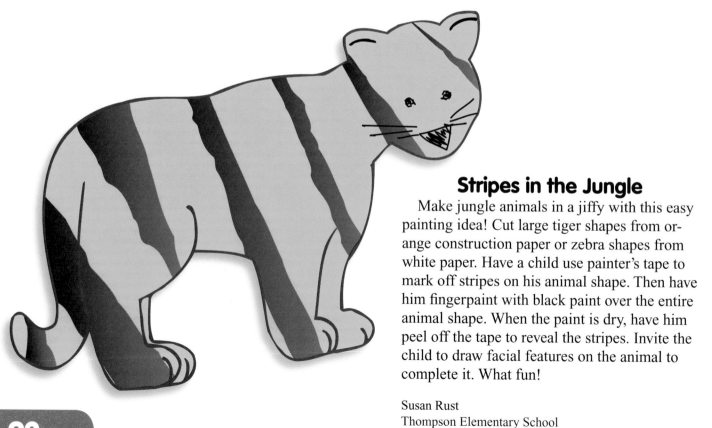

### Stripes in the Jungle

Make jungle animals in a jiffy with this easy painting idea! Cut large tiger shapes from orange construction paper or zebra shapes from white paper. Have a child use painter's tape to mark off stripes on his animal shape. Then have him fingerpaint with black paint over the entire animal shape. When the paint is dry, have him peel off the tape to reveal the stripes. Invite the child to draw facial features on the animal to complete it. What fun!

Susan Rust
Thompson Elementary School
Jacksonville, NC

## Pretty As a Peacock

The plumage on this pretty peacock is sure to please your preschoolers. To make a giant peacock, use large droppers to randomly drop yellow, blue, and purple tempera paints onto a piece of white bulletin-board paper. Dip a trim roller into a meat tray filled with green or blue paint; then roll it over the dots in an outward motion, creating a fan shape. When the paint is dry, complete the peacock by gluing a construction paper body to the base of the painting as shown.

Pat Johnson
Church of the Redeemer
Columbus, OH

## Precious Puppies

Think these dogs are cute? It must be puppy love! To make one, paint the bottom of a child's foot the color of his choice, such as white, brown, black, or gray. Have the child press a footprint onto a sheet of construction paper. When the paint is dry, provide the child with paper scraps, markers, and sticky dot-eyes for decorating his dog as he desires. Display these canine crafts so that everyone can "paws" to admire them!

Stephanie Adkison
Stillwater, OK

## "Tutti-Fruity"

Encourage your young sculptors to make these fruit bowls that look good enough to eat! First, provide each child with a portion of Crayola Model Magic modeling compound. Help her flatten it to a thickness of about one-half inch. Have her use cookie cutters to cut out a large circle, a small circle, and a small heart shape. Have her use a plastic knife to cut each circle in half; then set her pieces on a paper plate to dry. When the shapes are dry, direct the child to paint the larger half circles orange, the smaller ones yellow, and the heart shape red. Then assist her in adding lines of white paint to the half circles so they resemble orange and lemon wedges. Have her add white paint dots to the heart shape so it resembles a straw-berry. Then display all the finished pieces in a small paper or plastic bowl. Yum!

Christy J. McClellan
Song Woods School
Waynesboro, PA

## Watercolor Orchids

To make an orchid, cut a sheet of white construction paper in half lengthwise. Drop a bit of green liquid watercolor paint onto one end of the paper. Have a child use a straw to blow the paint across the paper, creating long green "stems." Help him press a small circular sponge into a bright color of liquid watercolor and then dab "petals" onto the end of each stem. Oh my—orchids!

Tracy Karczewski
La Jolla Presbyterian Preschool
La Jolla, CA

## Vase of Violets

*V* is for *vase, violets,* and *very* fun! To begin, cut out one copy of the vase pattern on page 110 for each child. Have each child use crayons to practice writing the letter *V* on his vase. Then glue the vase near the bottom edge of a sheet of colorful construction paper. To make violets for the vase, tear a scrap of purple construction paper into small pieces. Place four or five dollops of glue above the vase and then press the torn paper into the glue. When the glue is dry, add stems and leaves with crayons. What a nice variety of violets!

Nancy McComas
Lord of Life Preschool
Memphis, TN

## Pansy Picture Frame

What will parents say about this pressed-pansy picture frame? "Wow! Impressive!" In advance, press a supply of pansy flowers in a heavy book for approximately one week. Cut out a tagboard picture frame for each child and have her paint a watercolor design on it. When the paint is dry, provide the child with a few pressed flowers and direct her to glue them onto the frame. Tape a photo of the child behind the frame. Laminate the frame and then add a strip of magnetic tape to the back of it. Pressed and complete! This picture frame can't be beat!

## Squirrel Patterns

Use with "Winter Preparations" on page 9.

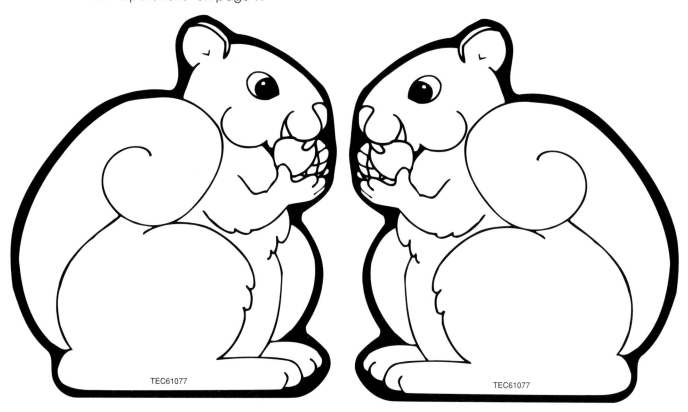

TEC61077

TEC61077

## Owl Patterns

Use with "Moonlit Autumn Trees" on page 10.

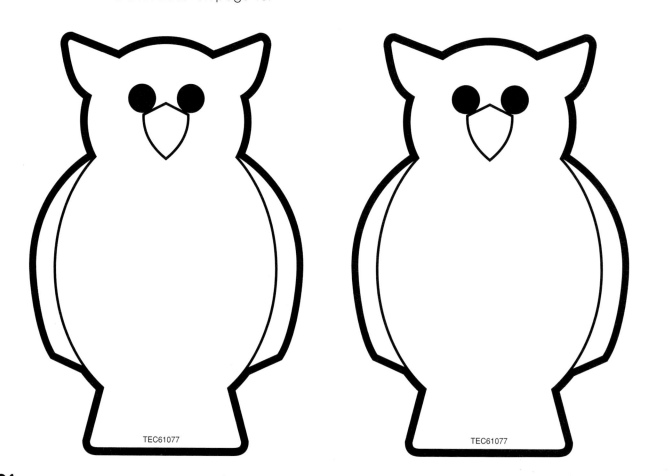

TEC61077

TEC61077

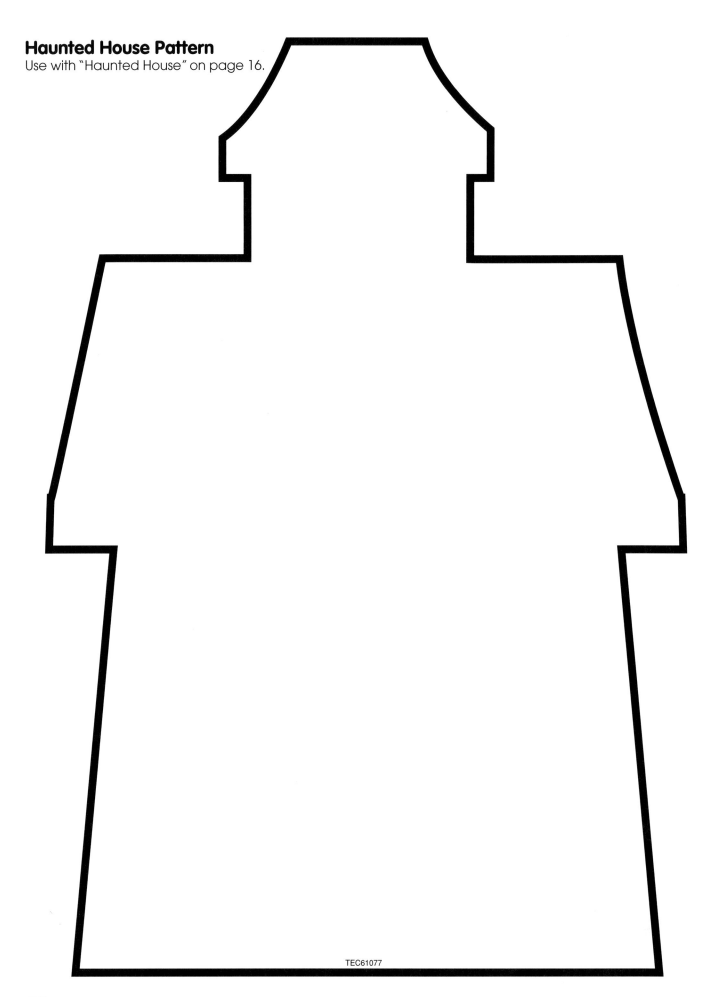

TEC61077

TEC61077

# Turkey Patterns

Use with "Flock of Turkeys" on page 21.

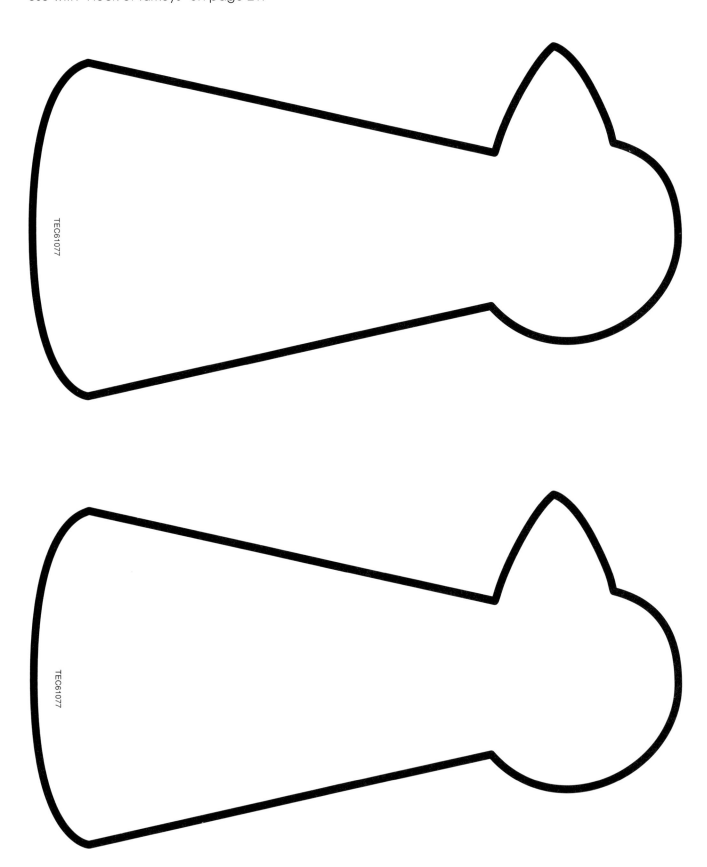

TEC61077

TEC61077

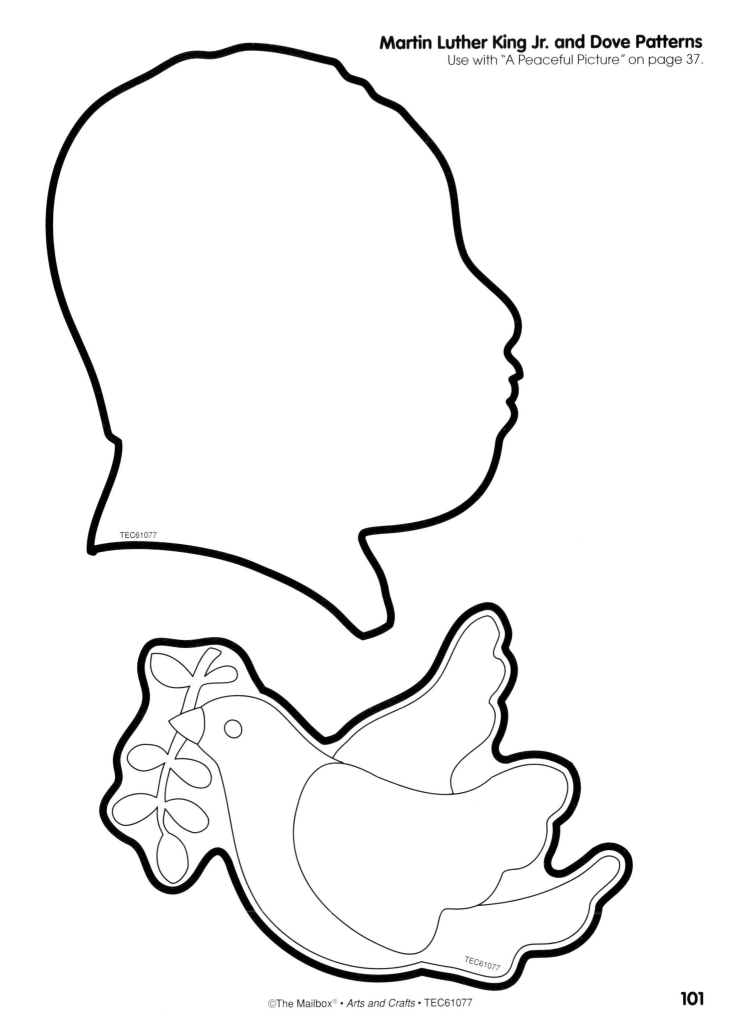

TEC61077

TEC61077

# Penguin Patterns
Use with "Paper Bag Penguin" on page 38.

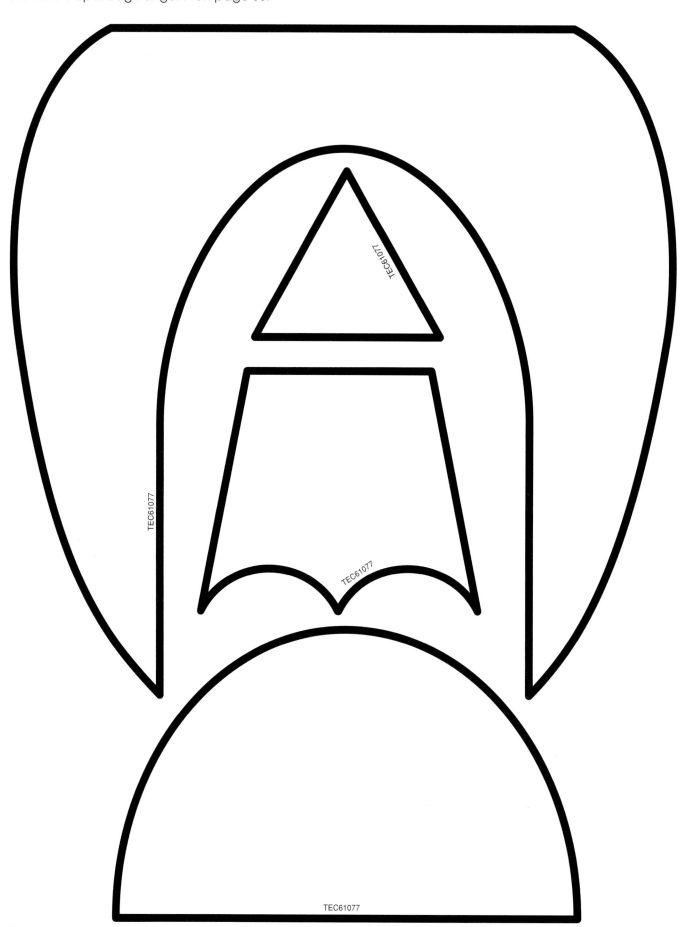

TEC61077

# Rabbit Pattern
Use with "Round and Round Rabbit" on page 53.

# Bow Tie Pattern
Use with "Bunny Frame" on page 53.

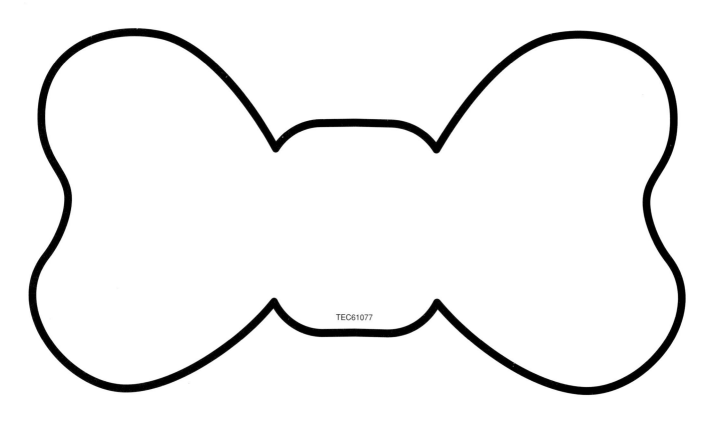

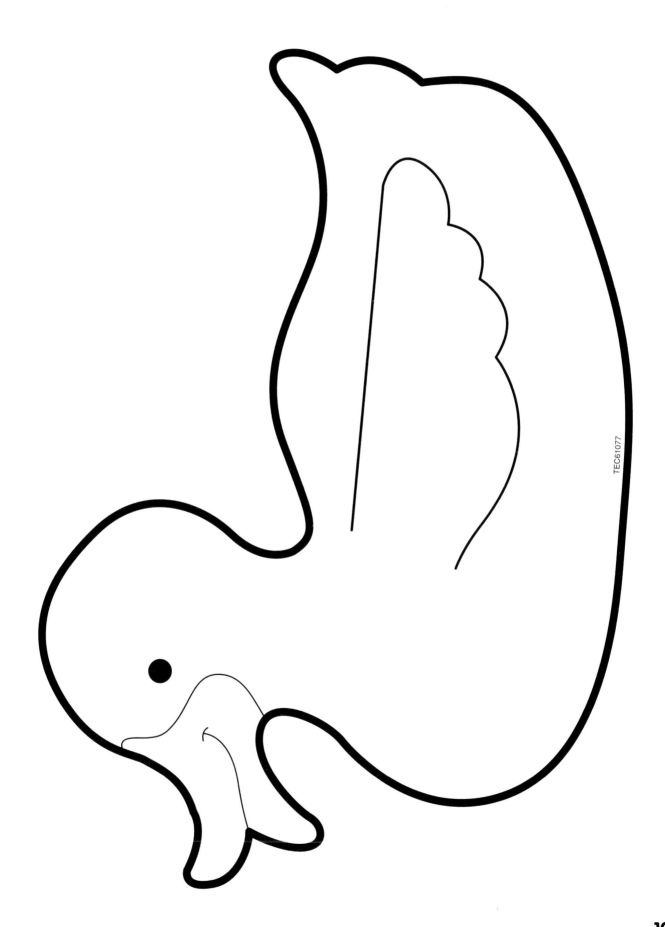

TEC61077

# Sunglasses Patterns
Use with "Beach Props" on page 71.

TEC61077

TEC61077

TEC61077

# Hat Pattern

Use with "Western Wear" on page 91.

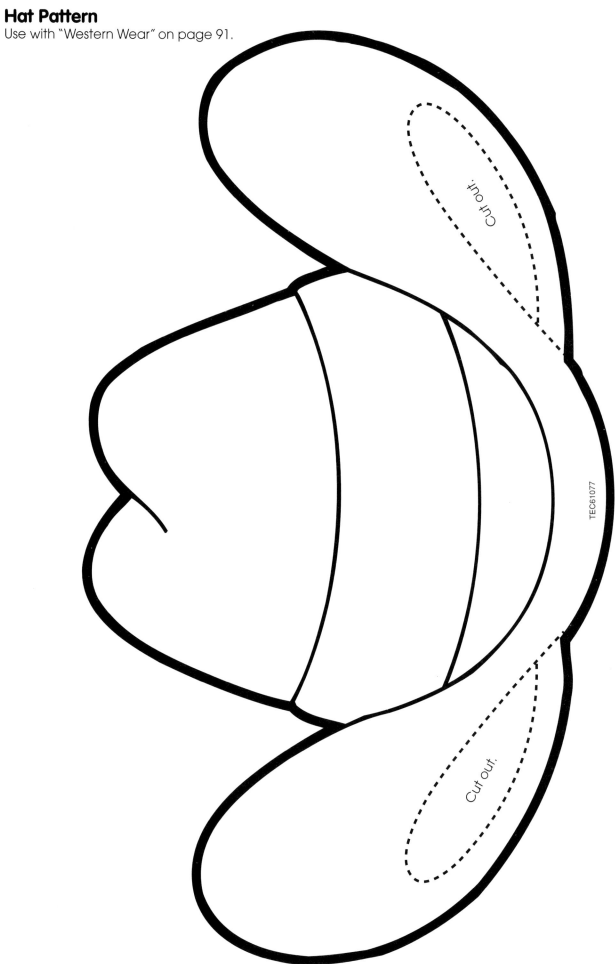

Cut out.

Cut out.

TEC61077

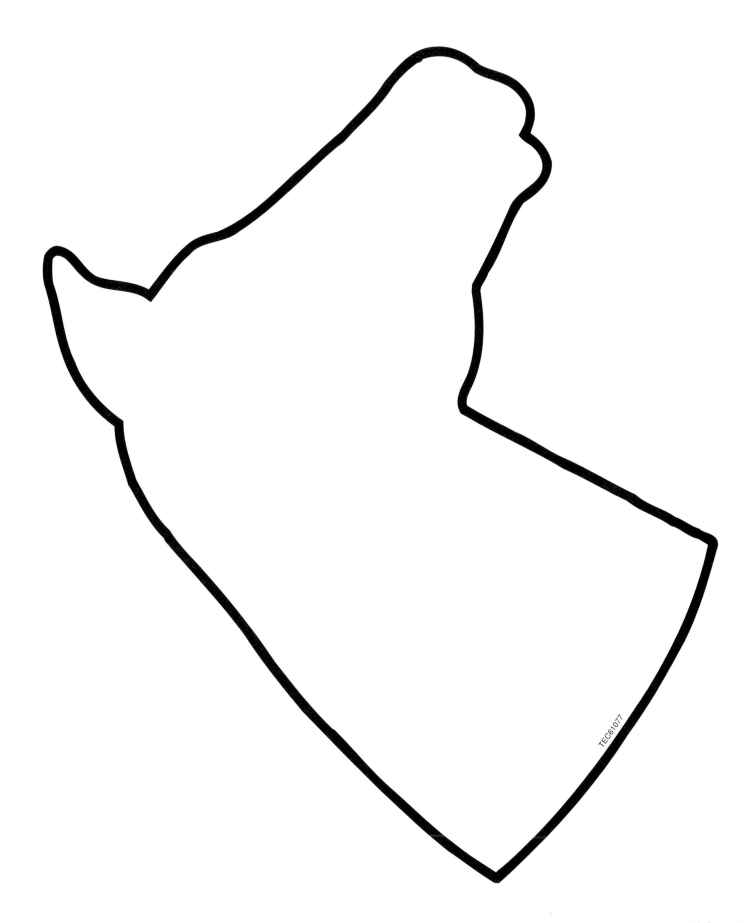

TEC61077

# Vase Pattern

Use with "Vase of Violets" on page 95.

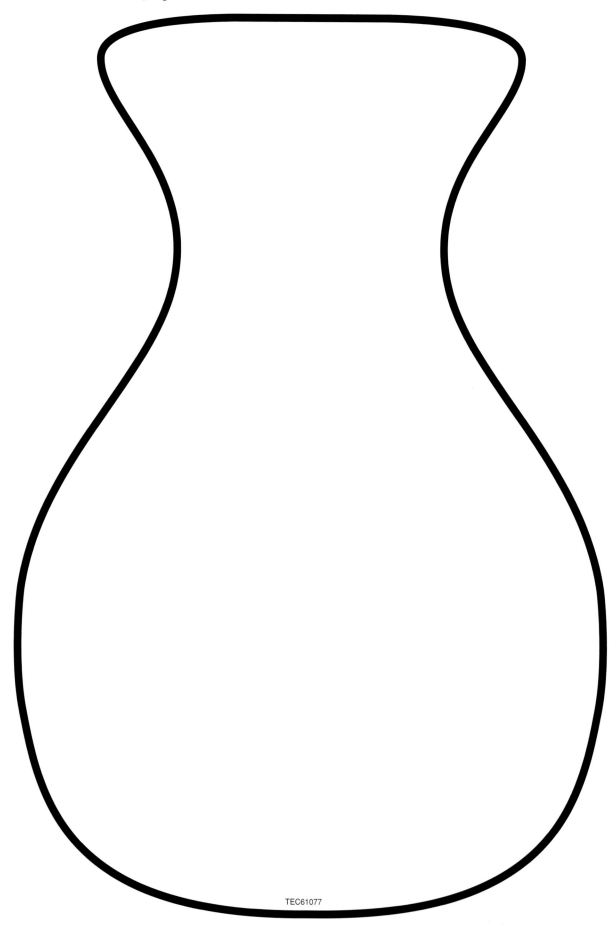

TEC61077

# Index